Cambridge Elements

Elements in New Religious Movements
Series Editor
Rebecca Moore
San Diego State University
Founding Editor
† James R. Lewis
Wuhan University

MANAGING RELIGION AND RELIGIOUS CHANGES IN IRAN

A Socio-Legal Analysis

Sajjad Adeliyan Tous
Independent Scholar
James T. Richardson
University of Nevada, Reno

CAMBRIDGE
UNIVERSITY PRESS

CAMBRIDGE UNIVERSITY PRESS

Shaftesbury Road, Cambridge CB2 8EA, United Kingdom

One Liberty Plaza, 20th Floor, New York, NY 10006, USA

477 Williamstown Road, Port Melbourne, VIC 3207, Australia

314–321, 3rd Floor, Plot 3, Splendor Forum, Jasola District Centre, New Delhi – 110025, India

103 Penang Road, #05–06/07, Visioncrest Commercial, Singapore 238467

Cambridge University Press is part of Cambridge University Press & Assessment, a department of the University of Cambridge.

We share the University's mission to contribute to society through the pursuit of education, learning and research at the highest international levels of excellence.

www.cambridge.org
Information on this title: www.cambridge.org/9781009460118

DOI: 10.1017/9781009460095

When citing this work, please include a reference to the DOI 10.1017/9781009460095

First published 2024

A catalogue record for this publication is available from the British Library.

ISBN 978-1-009-46011-8 Hardback
ISBN 978-1-009-46007-1 Paperback
ISSN 2635-232X (online)
ISSN 2635-2311 (print)

Managing Religion and Religious Changes in Iran

A Socio-Legal Analysis

Elements in New Religious Movements

DOI: 10.1017/9781009460095
First published online: May 2024

Sajjad Adeliyan Tous
Independent Scholar

James T. Richardson
University of Nevada, Reno

Author for correspondence: Sajjad Adeliyan Tous, sjd.adeliyan@gmail.com

Abstract: This Element offers a theoretically informed examination of the manner in which religion, especially alternative and emergent religious and spiritual movements, is managed by law and legal mechanisms in the authoritarian theocracy of Iran. It highlights how these phenomena have been affected by the intersection of law, politics, and Shiʿi theology in recent Iranian history. The growing interest of Iranian citizens in new religious movements and spiritual currents, fostered by the cultural diffusion of Western writings and ideas, is described. The development of religious diversity in Iran and a corresponding loss of commitment toward some Islamic doctrines and practices are of considerable concern to both the Iranian religious and political establishments. This has led to social control efforts over any religious and spiritual movement differing from the regime's view of Islam. Those efforts, supported in large part by Western anticult ideas, culminated in the passage of a piece of stringent legislation in 2021. The Element closes with applications of theorizing from the sociology of law and of religion.

Keywords: Iran, authoritarian regimes, regulation of religion, religious discrimination and persecution, religious minorities, new religious movements, spiritual currents, cults

ISBNs: 9781009460118 (HB), 9781009460071 (PB), 9781009460095 (OC)
ISSNs: 2635-232X (online), 2635-2311 (print)

Contents

Introduction and Relevant Background

> The magistrate ought not to forbid the preaching or professing of any speculative opinions in any Church because they have no manner of relation to the civil rights of the subjects. If a Roman Catholic believe that to be really the body of Christ which another man calls bread, he does no injury thereby to his neighbour. If a Jew do not believe the New Testament to be the word of God, he does not thereby alter anything in men's civil rights. If a heathen doubt of both Testaments, he is not therefore to be punished as a pernicious citizen. The power of the magistrate and the estates of the people may be equally secure, whether any man believe these things or no. I readily grant that these opinions are false and absurd. But the business of laws is not to provide for the truth of opinions, but for the safety and security of the commonwealth, and of every particular man's goods and person.
>
> –John Locke, *A Letter Concerning Toleration*, 1689

Much has been written concerning the disheartening rise of "authoritarianism" in the modern world, given impetus by the growing prevalence of authoritarian (*iqtidār-girā*)[1] regimes around the globe. Some of that attention has been on Muslim nations that have adopted versions of Islam to promote and maintain their governments.[2] "With the help of the religious bureaucracy, state-sponsored Islam produces an orthodox, conformist version of Islam ['state Islam' or 'official Islam'] that endeavors to legitimize the prevailing regime and support its strategic choices policies" (Hmimnat 2021: 1).[3] Much of that literature, however, has been based on analyses that are historical in nature or that adopt a perspective derived mainly from political science (e.g., Karawan 1992; Hakim 1998; Omelicheva 2016; Sheikh and Ahmed 2020). This Element focuses attention on theoretical traditions from the sociology of religion and the sociology of law to address developments in the realm of the phenomenon of religion and spirituality in one such country, Iran. Undoubtedly, such regimes must often grapple with competition from newer religious and spiritual ideas

[1] We adhered herein to the conventions of the *International Journal of Middle East Studies* (*IJMES*) for transliterations.

[2] Addressing the question of "why do Muslim-majority countries exhibit high levels of authoritarianism and low levels of socio-economic development in comparison to world averages?" Kuru (2019) criticizes explanations that point to Islam as the cause of this disparity. He argues that Muslims had influential thinkers and merchants in their early history when religious orthodoxy and military rule were prevalent in Europe. However, in the eleventh century, an alliance between orthodox *'ulamā'* and military states began to emerge. This alliance gradually hindered intellectual and economic creativity by marginalizing members of the intellectual and bourgeois classes in the Muslim world. Kuru's study links its historical explanation to contemporary politics by showing that, to this day, the *'ulamā'*–state alliance still prevents creativity and competition in Muslim countries. See Grim and Finke (2011), especially chapter 6, "What about Muslim-Majority Countries?" for a discussion of Saudi Arabia and Iran and the quite authoritarian implementation of versions of Shariʿa law. See also Fox (2016, 2020) for more details about how authoritarian societies, including Islamic ones, control religion.

[3] This process is authoritarian in essence since it tends to concentrate and vest religious authority in the hands of the government.

and movements. Of course, not all Muslim governments are authoritarian and restrict religious freedom. Philpott (2019) divides the Muslim world's states into three categories: religiously free states (e.g., Senegal and Sierra Leone), secular repressive states (e.g., Uzbekistan and Egypt), and religiously repressive states (e.g., Iran and Saudi Arabia). Sarkissian (2015) also specifically identifies three classifications of regimes practicing religious repression: states that repress all religious groups, countries that repress all religious groups but one, and nations that selectively repress some religious groups.

Iran is a theocratic polity characterized by Shiʿite clerical governance with the assumed superiority and hegemony of Shariʿa[4] and state enforcement of an Iranian version of Islam.[5] It furnishes an instructive example of how such authoritarian governments manage religion, including traditional minority faiths as well as new religious movements (NRMs) and spiritual currents.[6] Indeed, present-day Iran is a prototypical case of an authoritarian regime based on a specific interpretation of Islam that seems designed mainly to guarantee the continuation of the government that evolved out of the 1979 Iranian Revolution. This mirrors the "political activism" approach within Shiʿa Islam, developed in

---

[4] There is no single meaning of the term "Shariʿa," but powerful emotional and political connotations are now associated with its use – and abuse. Shariʿa has been transformed from a path, to God's perfect law, to an invocation of identity against the Other (Gunn and Sabil 2023).

[5] An-Naʿim (2009) argues that the future of Shariʿa, the normative system of Islam, lies among believers and their communities, not in the enforcement of its principles by the coercive power of the state. By its nature and purposes, Shariʿa, he contends, can be freely observed only by believers, and its principles lose their religious authority and value when enforced by the state. He calls this theory "the religious neutrality of the state," whereby state institutions neither favor nor disfavor any religious doctrine or principle. The object of this neutrality, however, is precisely the freedom of Muslims in their communities to live by their own belief in Islam while other citizens live by their own beliefs. For An-Naʿim, the institutional separation of Islam and the state is of the essence for Shariʿa to have its proper positive role in the lives of Muslims and Islamic societies.

[6] In order to discuss the groups commonly referred to as cults while avoiding that term, scholars have employed several alternatives, the most common of which is "new religious movements," which has gained a strong foothold in the sociology of religion (Olson 2006: 98; see also Richardson 1993a and Dillon and Richardson 1994 for critiques of the term *cult*). Eileen Barker offers a nonevaluative and objective definition of an NRM: "The term . . . is used to cover a disparate collection of organisations, most of which have emerged in their present form since the 1950s, and most of which offer some kind of answer to questions of a fundamental religious, spiritual or philosophical nature" (1989: 9). Herein we use a variety of terms with the same meaning as NRM. We also use *cult* in some places herein only because of its appearance in Iranian official documents. An NRM may be one of a wide range of movements ranging from those with loose affiliations based on novel approaches to spirituality or religion to communitarian enterprises that demand a considerable amount of group conformity and a social identity that separates their adherents from mainstream society. However innovative they may be, NRMs always utilize elements of earlier religious traditions as building blocks to construct their new theologies, practices, and organizations. Contemporary NRMs have attracted mainly younger adherents who seek alternatives to traditional religious views and organizations extant in their societies.

the latter half of the twentieth century by the Najaf-trained *faqīhs* Muhammad Baqir al-Sadr and Ruhollah Khomeini: it is for the juristic class to seize the reins of power directly and enact positive state law themselves on the basis of the rules derived by the *faqīhs* over the centuries.[7] Such a legal system might not be ideal in the absence of the infallible Imam, given the very real possibility of juristic errors and omissions in interpretation. However, it is argued that this should not deter trying to establish a legal system based on ideal Islamic law during Imam Mahdi's occultation.[8]

This Element describes and analyzes the years-long government-based religious discrimination (GRD) and efforts to regulate religion in Iran. Fox defines GRD as "restrictions placed by governments or their agents on the religious practices or institutions of religious minorities that are not placed on the majority religion" (2020: 10). Referring to the actions of the state that deny religious freedoms or inhibit their full realization and flourishing, Grim and Finke define governmental regulation of religion as "any laws, policies, or administrative actions that impinge on the practice, profession, or selection of religion" (2006: 13). These regulatory efforts have particularly affected the growing interest in newer religious and spiritual movements of various kinds that have developed in Iran. It is argued that seemingly benign and legal forms of regulations, requirements, and restrictions on religion are important tools by which nondemocratic leaders repress independent civic activity and thus hold on to their power. Human rights violations, specifically in regard to religious freedom, are disputed and

[7] "[T]he denial of legitimacy to existing forms of government during the period of *ghaiba* lends itself to at least two possible interpretations – one leading to quietism in the absence of the Twelfth Imam and the other to activism" (Bahar 1992: 162). "Quietism" is the more long-standing approach. By the quietist political theory, perfect justice and peace can be established only upon the eventual reappearance of an infallible Hidden Imam, the Mahdi (pbuh), whose name is invoked by the faithful and who is called upon by them to emerge from his concealment. To the quietist, the best approach to state law is to endure it as one endures all ordeals, follow God's law as closely as might be feasible, and await the Mahdi's return. It is no ideal state of affairs, to be sure, but a divinely ordained one that God will choose one day to end by ordering the Hidden Imam to reappear to establish perfect justice. After all, "both [approaches] manage to retain some sense of purity and logic as concerns the relationship of state law to Islamic law, and they do this by delegitimizing state law and indeed the state itself, to the extent that the state departs from Islamic law norms" (Ala Hamoudi 2019: 303).

[8] Plainly, in both cases, ideal justice is provided only by the implementation of Islamic law, not a law of the state that is inconsistent with Islamic law. But having said that, "[t]he . . . difference between the two approaches relates to *who* has the authority to implement religious law, and *what* is to be done when other rules happen to prevail. For the Quietist, only the Mahdi may implement the law because, among other things, only the Mahdi fully knows it. For the juristic revolutionaries, the jurists may implement it as best as they can on behalf of the state in their role as deputies in the Mahdi's absence, pending his return" (Ala Hamoudi 2019: 303, italics in original). That being so, quietists disagree with activists over the governance of clergymen and control of social life based on religious injunctions during the age of occultation (*ʿaṣr-i ghaybat*) of the infallible Imam.

politicized (see Afshari 2011: 147–50), resulting in the Iranian rule sometimes being portrayed as "Islamofascist" (Amirpur 2012).[9] This is why the United Nations (UN) Special Rapporteur referred to the investigation of human rights in Iran as "particularly complex and complicated," which is "one of the most controversial of all the mandates on which international monitoring has focused in particular countries" (UN Doc. 1991a: 90). Nonetheless, this controversy has gone on in "prejudiced and speculative terms, which have been accompanied by reactions of hypersensitivity" (91), ergo, it needs to be explored, taking a scientific approach. We hope to contribute to such an effort.

Section 1 of this Element explores key provisions within the Iranian Constitution that are germane to the treatment of minority faiths and other religious and spiritual movements within Iran, hence demonstrating the internally contradictory nature of the Constitution and also the clear primacy of Islam in the document. Section 2 describes how non-Muslim religious groups have been defined and treated within the Islamic government of Iran. Section 3 is devoted to the discussion of major cultural shifts that have occurred (and are continuing) in Iran among the general public in how they approach religious and spiritual issues. The influence of Western ideas about newer religious and spiritual phenomena is analyzed, as is the rise of unapproved derivatives of Islam that have grown in popularity. These developments have led to considerable disquiet among Iranian clerics and political authorities. In Section 4, we present in considerable detail efforts over the years to generate new legislation for the government to exercise social control over NRMs in Iran. This controversial attempt finally came to fruition in 2021 with the adoption of a major change in the Iranian criminal statute – the additional Article 500 *bis* – that can facilitate social control of minority faiths and NRMs of all types. In Section 5, we close our Element with a discussion of specific applications of sociologically oriented theoretical perspectives to what has happened in Iran and, by implication, what may be occurring in other authoritarian Islamic regimes. Before presenting details of the situation in Iran, we offer some useful background information that includes a brief commentary on the right to freedom of religion or belief (FoRB).

Religious Freedom

"Religious freedom" or "freedom of religion or belief" is a relatively new and socially constructed term brought about in a context of historical and societal conditions that made the conceptual development of the term an apparently

[9] Identifying the essence or core tenets of "fascism" and considering whether or not a generic label of it may be extended to other similar regimes is an area of semantic, theoretical, and ideological disagreement. Today, fascism has become a general, pejorative term for any system or exercise of power contested for apparently dictatorial qualities.

pragmatic solution to major events (Richardson 2006). These include (1) unending warfare in seventeenth-century Europe – the Thirty Years' War, ending in 1648 and leading to the Treaty of Westphalia; (2) the inability of one religious group to dominate the newly formed United States, leading to the First Amendment of the US Constitution with its religious freedom and anti-establishment clauses; (3) the tragedy of World War II, which led to the establishment of the Council of Europe (COE) and the European Convention on Human Rights and Fundamental Freedoms (ECHR) with its famous Article 9 guaranteeing freedom of thought, conscience, and religion; and (4) the breakup of the Soviet Union leading to the flood of nations wanting to affiliate with the COE, contributing to the enforcement of Article 9 guaranteeing freedom of thought, conscience, and religion by the European Court of Human Rights (ECtHR) for the first time in 1993 (Richardson 1995; Evans 2001). These four historical occurrences are watershed events in the social construction of religious freedom.

Religious freedom is comprised of two elements of "belief" (*forum internum*) and "manifestation" (*forum externum*) (Gunner 2023). The *forum internum* dimension (i.e., freedom to have or to adopt a religion or belief of one's choice) is "absolutely protected" (UN Doc. 2014: 7) under Article 4(2) of the International Covenant on Civil and Political Rights (ICCPR) and states cannot derogate from this aspect of the right of FoRB even when the life of the nation is at stake. The *forum externum* dimension (i.e., freedom to manifest one's religion or belief in worship, observance, practice, and teaching), however, does not enjoy such powerful support and is not unqualifiedly immune from possible limitations (Van der Vyver 2005; Gunn 2011; Ahdar and Leigh 2013; Ghanea and Pinto 2020; Raza 2020). True religious freedom is fulfilled with the union of its dual elements, which would be meaningless in the absence of (i.e., nonadherence to) either. Therefore, states should be expected to observe both elements if claims are made that FoRB exists in a society.

Much ink has been spilled in the name of and in defense of the right to religious freedom, and many have waxed eloquently about its virtues, even if guarantees found in constitutions are sometimes honored in the breach (Fox and Flores 2009; Finke and Mataic 2019; Mataic and Finke 2019; Fox 2023). Nonetheless, 162 countries out of 183 (88.5 percent) in the Religion and State data set engage in religious discrimination by placing at least one of the thirty-six types of limitations on at least one religious minority, repressing religious freedom-related rights in some way (Fox 2018: 160). Religious discrimination and persecution are far more serious in authoritarian and totalitarian regimes and correspondingly religious freedom is often experiencing crisis in those settings.

Jonathan Fox (2015, 2016) has proposed that religious freedom should be considered in terms of normative principles of liberty and equality and related to the concepts of political secularism and state–religion governance. Political secularism can be defined as "an ideology or set of beliefs that advocates that religion ought to be separate from all or some aspects of politics and/or public life" (Fox 2017: 103). It is clear in our study that political secularism does not exist in Iran and that, indeed, clerical and political leaders in Iran have exerted considerable effort over the decades since the Revolution to make sure that a specific version of Islam permeates every aspect of Iranian culture and life. This has led to considerable difficulties for all religious groups and spiritual movements that vary from the officially approved version of Islam.

1 Religion and Religious Freedom in Iran's Post-Revolutionary Constitution

Francis Fukuyama asserts that the Constitution of the Islamic Republic of Iran, adopted after the 1979 Revolution (and last amended in 1989), is "a curious hybrid of authoritarian, theocratic and democratic elements" (quoted in Jahanbegloo 2011: 129). The Iranian Constitution exhibits "Pro-Center Dogmatic Authoritarianism and Pro-Persian Cosmopolitanism" as the two foundations of Iran's political system (Asim 2023). It contains provisions that call for religious freedom, such as this statement in Article 23: "The investigation of the beliefs of a person is forbidden, and no one may be molested or prosecuted for holding a belief." There are also two more provisions stating that the Constitution recognizes some religions other than Islam and the Iranian state is obliged to deal with non-Muslims fairly:

> Article 13: Zoroastrians, Jews, and Christians among Iranians are the only recognized religious minorities who, within the limits of the law, are free to perform their religious rites and ceremonies and act in accordance with their own canon in matters of personal law and religious education.[10]
>
> Article 14: In accordance with the noble verse, "Allah does not forbid you to deal justly and kindly with those who fought not against you on account of religion nor drove you out of your homes" [Q al-Mumtaḥana 60:8], the government of the Islamic Republic of Iran and the Muslims are required to treat non-Muslims with good moral manners and Islamic justice and equity,

[10] "Although the majority of [the] Iranian population follows the Twelver sect of Shiʿa Islam, the Iranian Constitution also recognizes [the] Hanafi, Shafi'i, Maliki, and Hanbali sects of Sunni Islam and the Zaidi sect of Shiʿa Islam as the only officially acceptable branches of Islam within the territorial jurisdiction of Iran [see Article 12 of the Constitution]. Other than the respective sects, the Constitution neither recognizes nor gives constitutional privilege to Ismaʿili Shiʿa, Baha'i, Yarsani (Ahl-e Haqq), and Darvish (Sufi) communities. The case is the same for followers of Mandaeism, Hinduism, and Sikhism" (Asim 2023: 18–19).

> and observe their human rights. This article applies to those who do not plot and act against Islam and the Islamic Republic of Iran.

The term "Islamic justice and equity" in Article 14 means that Islamic law shapes the rights of non-Muslims. Far from granting non-Muslims protections for the rights to which they are entitled under international law, the Constitution reinforces the principle that their human rights are subject to Iran's version of Islamic criteria. Other lines in Article 14 reveal that the drafters presumed that non-Muslims are inclined to act against Islam and are disposed to be disloyal to Iran's Islamic Republic. Given the bias in the Iranian constitutional system, such things would seem only natural. Having promised Islamic justice to non-Muslims, the limited human rights that non-Muslims supposedly enjoy are to be forfeited when conspiracies against the state are assumed – a vague standard affording a broad range of justifications for curbing their rights. Mayer writes in the analysis of Article 14:

> Significantly, this article provides special grounds for depriving non-Muslims of human rights in addition to the curbs that are provided in Article 26, which enables the government to curb the activities of groups, including "minority religious associations," if they are "contrary to the principles of Islam or the Islamic Republic." Together, Articles 14 and 26 set up the basis for depriving minorities of rights and freedoms for being against the principles of Islam and the Islamic Republic. (2018: 143–4)

Moreover, Articles 13, 14, and 23 are preempted or contradicted by the substantial Preamble to the Constitution (see Ramazani 1980: 184–7) and other provisions (e.g., Article 1) that make it plain that Iran is an *Islamic* country with quite limited religious freedom for minority religious communities. The existence of such contradictions and the foundational tensions they reflect call for an urgent and candid discussion of the problem. The Iranian principle and practice of a democratic republic is secondary and subordinate to Islamic criteria. Notwithstanding the Constitution's ostensible recognition of universal human rights, the overarching and ultimate hallmark and benchmark of rights under the Constitution is captured and constrained by the phrase "Islamic criteria" and is subject to clerical interpretation. Article 4 of the Constitution prescribes:

> All civil, penal, financial, economic, administrative, cultural, military, political, and other laws and regulations must be based on Islamic criteria. This principle applies absolutely and generally to all articles of the Constitution and other laws and regulations, and the *fuqahā*ʾ of the Guardian Council are judges in this matter.

Indeed, by positioning this article prior to other articles, the framers of the Constitution symbolically emphasized that a specific religion forms the basis for government action in Iran. In this regard, Gouda and Gutmann (2021) examine the effects of constitutions prescribing Shariʿa as a source of legislation on discrimination against religious minorities. Their empirical analysis shows that religious minorities in countries where the status and supremacy of Shariʿa is entrenched constitutionally are likely to face more discrimination than they do elsewhere:[11]

> First, the level of Islamization of a country's constitution is significantly associated with minority discrimination. Second, after considering the possible entrenchment of Islamic legal principles in the constitution, the effect of any other measure of Islam's influence on the level of religious minority discrimination no longer is significant. In other words, the widespread prevalence of religious minority discrimination in Muslim societies seems to be a consequence of the design of formal institutions (i.e., especially the constitution) rather than caused directly by widespread adherence to Islam. That finding aligns with the more general idea that constitutions matter. (2021: 258)

The study by Gouda and Gutmann has demonstrated once more the grave menace of institutionalizing supreme values, be they communist or Islamic. Constitutions that propagate absolute truths and expect all members of society to adhere to those principles are inherently incompatible with the protection of minority rights. However, declaring that the state has an official religion can mean many things, ranging from a symbolic connection with no practical implications to a state governed by a specific religious law. While the official religion clauses and practical commitment are correlated, it is only *actual* levels of state support for religion consistently, significantly, and strongly that predict GRD (Fox 2023). Thus, government backing of religion, as reflected in laws, governmental practices, and court rulings, is the key measure of a state's relationship with religion that influences GRD.

Islamic constitutions can be quite problematic for minority religious groups when they are interpreted directly by courts as criminalizing certain actions by such groups, but also when they furnish the legal foundation for legislation curtailing the rights and freedoms of minorities. Sharply contrasted with high degrees of autonomy are situations where the courts serve only at the pleasure of rulers, with their functionaries appointed by such entities. One only needs to contemplate a country such as Iran to grasp this point. Judges in Iran understand that they have little autonomy and that if they choose to exercise independent judgment, their jobs may be jeopardized (UN Doc. 2022: 16). Judges under such a system realize that they are to assist in implementing the ideology and maintaining the omnipotence of the Establishment. "[O]nly a male candidate who has faith and is deemed just and in possession of 'a practical commitment

[11] However, they find no evidence suggesting that Islam encourages discrimination against minorities when it is not entrenched in the constitution.

to Islamic principles and loyalty to the system of the Islamic Republic' may be considered as a judge or a prosecutor" (Banakar and Ziaee 2018: 723). Along the same line, a major form of potential risk against religious freedom appears when Islamic constitutions empower the courts of law to find persons guilty solely on the basis of Islamic rules, whereas there is no legal basis for the criminality of the attributed accusation (lack of the *élément légal*). An example from the Iranian Constitution is:

> Article 167: A judge shall be required to try to find out the verdict of every lawsuit in codified laws; if he fails to find out, he shall render a judgment on the matter under consideration based on *authentic Islamic sources* or *authoritative fatāwā*. He may not refrain from dealing with the case and rendering a judgment on the pretext of silence, inadequacy, or brevity of or contradiction in codified laws. (italics added)

Even though no explicit statutory provision criminalizes abandonment of Islam or conversion from it, converts regularly receive death penalty threats under the classical jurisprudential charge of "apostasy," invoking Article 167 of the Constitution.[12] For instance, branch 11 of the Appeal and Criminal Court of Gilan province, in decision No. 8909971314400980, dated 22 September 2010, found an Iranian citizen who converted to Christianity at the age of nineteen guilty as *murtadd-i fiṭrī*.[13] The court condemned him to execution, citing Article 167 and fatwas of several Shiʿa *faqīh*s, notably Ayatollah Khomeini and the Supreme Leader Ayatollah Khamenei. However, this judgment was subsequently overturned by decision No. 212, dated 12 June 2011, of branch 27 of the Supreme Court of Iran because it was determined that inquiries into his life and beliefs were defective:

> While the convict Mr. Youcef Nadarkhani has been confessor [*muʿtarif*] to heartily and practically leaving the holy religion of Islam, and believing in Christianity, and preaching in this direction, and some persons' leaving Islam and entering Christianity as the result of his preachings, and adopting the pastoral role of the church, and insisting on Christianity, and not believing in the finality and prophethood of the Prophet Muhammad (pbuh), and denying the imamate of the Twelve Infallible Imams [*Aʾimmih*] (pbut), and not believing in the truthfulness [*ḥaqqānīyat*] of the collection of qurʾanic verses . . ., but in relation to the actualization [*taḥaqquq*] of apostasy, the verification of his Muslimhood after attaining puberty and the expression [*iẓhār*] of Islam and practical behavior in line

[12] For debates and controversies about "apostasy" in Shiʿa *fiqh*, see Kadivar (2021).

[13] "An apostate, defined as a Muslim who leaves Islam for unbelief or another religion, is considered either a *fiṭrī* or a *millī* apostate. The first one signifies that he had one Muslim parent at the time of his conception, expressed his belief in Islam after attaining maturity or reaching puberty (*bulūgh*), and renounced Islam later on. The second one signifies one whose parents were unbelievers at the time of his conception, had expressed his own unbelief (*kufr*) after having attained maturity, but at some point became Muslim and, later on, returned to unbelief" (Kadivar 2021: 26).

> with the Islamic teachings is necessary [for the court], and, in this regard, any investigation of local informants, acquaintances, relatives, and Muslims who have previously associated with him has not been conducted; thus, the investigations are incomplete. It is obvious that based on the *fatāwī* of eminent *fuqahā'*, including Imam Khomeini in the book *Taḥrīr al-Wasīla* . . ., the investigation into the expression of Islam is required: in case of proof of failure to express Islam [after pubescence and converting to Christianity], he should be asked to repent [*istitāba*], and in case of proof of expressing Islam [after pubescence and converting to Christianity], or with the nonoccurrence and absence [*intifā'*] of that and [the convict's] non-repentance, the death sentence be issued [for the latter two cases].

Iranian legal scholars have frequently criticized the controversial and awkward Article 167 since it transgresses the consensual principle of "legality," that is to say the legal maxim of *nullum crimen, nulla poena sine lege.*[14] Of greater concern is the association of apostasy with crimes against the state. Schirazi's interpretation of the scope of apostasy laws in contemporary Iran is that "apostates . . . are threatened with the harshest of punishments, namely the death penalty, a threat which may be carried out suddenly at any moment that suits the interests of the hierocracy" (1997: 139). Herein the punishment can be seen not only as a criminal justice deterrent instrument but also as subject to being manipulated by the government in order to enforce conformity.

In Article 13, the key phrases are "within the limits of the law" and the limitation "in matters of personal law and religious education." The Constitution and various laws make clear that nothing should impede the Islamic nature of the Islamic Republic of Iran, as defined by the clerics who oversee and control the government. Of course, even those two exceptions have been severely limited for the three *approved* faiths listed in Article 13. Other NRMs are more drastically controlled or even defined as illegal (e.g., Mysticism of the Ring[15] and the Ahmad al-Hassan al-

[14] See Tellenbach (2013) for detailed discussions surrounding Article 167.

[15] For example, in decision No. 26/19/94, dated 29 August 2015, branch 26 of the Islamic Revolutionary Court of Tehran sentenced a citizen to a one-year prison term for "insult to Islamic sanctities by membership and coaching in the ring of the false mysticism of cosmic consciousness and promoting and teaching the cult's thoughts and taking tuition fees in exchange for it" and to seventy-four lashes for "disturbance of public order by participating in unlawful assemblies in support of the convict Mohammad-Ali Taheri in front of Evin prison," as well as to pay 6 million rials in favor of the state for "acquiring illegitimate property." The court order also asserted that "she has attended illegal classes of the Ring Mysticism in Tehran actively and indeed is considered to be the representative of Tabriz in the cult. She has encouraged and aroused others to participate in the classes. She has been responsible for organizing and directing the Ring organization [*tashkīlāt-i Halgheh*] in Tabriz and is regarded as a main element of the cult." After an appeal against the judgment of the court of first instance, branch 36 of the Appeals Court of Tehran not only upheld the conviction but also declared the appellant's staying in Tabriz forbidden for two years as a complementary punishment "given her record and activity as an instructor [in the said group]" (decision No. 9509970223600272, dated 21 September 2016).

Yamānī movement[16]). The limitations indicated mean that activities other than education and personal law are strictly verboten (e.g., proselytizing). For example, branch 101 of the Criminal Court of Golpayegan, in decision No. 9209973720700356, dated 13 May 2013, sentenced a Sufi citizen to seventy-four lashes, invoking Article 167 and the book *Taḥrīr al-Wasīla*. He was charged with "committing the *ḥarām* act by promoting the beliefs of the Gonabadi Sufi cult." The defendant made reference to the constitutional protection of the right to freedom of expression in his defense before the court, but the judge dismissed it: "The scope of freedom is, not harming the rights of others and not infringing the Shariʿa principles and rules, and no one can, by having recourse to freedom, provide for the assault on individual rights and the Shariʿa sanctities."

This analysis of the demanding features and interpretations of the Iranian Constitution notwithstanding, we will now offer an assessment of minority religions' situation in Iran before discussing dramatic changes that have occurred (and are continuing) with the religious and spiritual life of Iranian citizens.

2 Religious Freedom Status of Minority Religious Groups in Iran: An Overview

Muslim popular prejudice and Islamic authority have always had difficulty accommodating new religions that arose after the dawn of Islam, especially those that emerged from within Muslim society and have developed separate traditions and communities of their own, often with a global expanse. For instance, Mirza Ghulam Ahmad (1835–1908) and Mirza Husayn-ʿAli Nuri (known as Bahāʾu'llāh) (1817–1892), who perceived themselves to be messianic individuals on a divinely sanctioned mission to herald a new millennium, are of particular significance, for their teachings led to the emergence of two highly

[16] For example, in case No. 14011140988, a seventeen-year-old juvenile was indicted for "propaganda activity against the *niẓām* [i.e., the ruling government and current political system in Iran] by promoting and propagating the thoughts and beliefs of the Yamānī deviant current and membership in the said cult" by the Tehran Special Prosecutor's Office of the Clergy. He was a recruit to one of the divisions of the Yamānī movement known as the Ahmadi Religion of Peace and Light. On 14 December 2022, the on-call/emergency judge (*qadī-yi kishīk*) of the Special Prosecutor's Office issued a bail in the sum of 5 billion rials, but since the accused was unable to deposit the money ordered, he was sent to the Correction and Rehabilitation Center of Tehran (i.e., a youth detention center). "The official function of the Special Court of the Clergy is to investigate criminal transgressions of the clergy, but the court has since the mid-1990s been used increasingly as an instrument for the suppression of dissident clerics, and at times even non-clerical culprits" (Künkler 2013: 57). In another case, branch 26 of the Islamic Revolutionary Court of Tehran, in decision No. 9809970262600102, dated 5 August 2019, sentenced a citizen to five years of incarceration due to the charge of "acting against the security of the country by membership in the illegal cult of Yamānī" and to a fine of 1,458,606 rials for "possessing prohibited goods (a deck of playing cards)." However, branch 36 of the Court of Appeals of Tehran province, while upholding the first instance court's verdict, reduced the jail sentence to two years (decision No. 9809970223600625, dated 18 November 2019).

controversial movements in modern Islamic history – the Ahmadiyya Jamāʿat and the Bahaʾi Faith. The Ahmadiyya movement claims to be a branch and sect of Islam, but its members have been officially declared non-Muslim in Pakistan and orthodox Muslims see them as unorthodox or *zindīq*. This has led to the widespread religious persecution of Ahmadis (Uddin 2013). Also, the presence of the post-qurʾanic monotheistic faith of Bahaʾism, defining itself as an independent religion, poses an unprecedented problem for Shariʿa (Pink 2003). From the *ʿulamā*'s point of view, Bahaʾis are kafirs, apostates, heretics, *najis*, Islamophobic, and the enemy of Islam because they have violated the theological idea of "the finality of prophethood" (*khātm-i Nubuwwat*). Bernard Lewis asserts: "The followers of such religions cannot be dismissed either as benighted heathens, like the polytheists of Asia and the animists of Africa, nor as outdated precursors, like the Jews and Christians, and their very existence presents a challenge to the Islamic doctrine of the perfection and finality of Muhammad's revelation" (2014: 20–1).

When contemporary Middle Eastern governments have pressed forward with Islamization campaigns, they have tended to impose a uniform standard of orthodoxy on their Muslim citizens and to reject the legitimacy of the positions of Muslim groups that do not accept what is being presented as the official norms of Islam. As the formal orthodoxy becomes identified with the regime's own ideology and legitimacy, modern governments have shown themselves inclined to label Muslims who do not accept the *official* Islam as heretics and apostates. According to some scholars:

> Although premodern Islamic culture was generally tolerant of diverging views on questions of Islamic theology and law, when contemporary Middle Eastern governments have espoused one official Islam or adopted Islamization programs, they have shown intolerance ... Thus, the ban on apostasy has become a means to criminalize what are deemed as heretical views, acting as a curb on the freedom of Muslims to follow a locally disfavored version of Islamic teachings. (Mayer 2018: 172)

Arzt (1995) contends that throughout Muslim history, and particularly in the contemporary era, much of the persecution of alleged apostates, heretics, and infidels has been politically motivated, designed to benefit controlling, orthodox groups who have resorted to religious justifications to legitimize their abusive power. In this regard, the notorious case of Nasr Hamid Abu Zayd (1943–2010), a Muslim intellectual and Cairo University professor, demonstrates that Egyptian courts were prepared to penalize progressive Islamic thought by classifying it as apostasy.[17] In fact, in many such contemporary cases, religious themes, doctrines, and rationales are intertwined with political slogans,

[17] For details of this case, see Najjar (2000) and Zainol, Abd Majid, and Kadir (2014).

motivations, and objectives. Often, a traditional religious veneer camouflages a politically motivated or radically violent core. Since Islam, especially as some clerics in Iran interpret it, makes no real distinction between state and religion, or between community politics and Shariʿa law, it may be impossible to separate out these influences.[18] The power of state-sanctioned legislation and judicial decision-making (or fatwa-issuing clergy) can be used to accomplish dual purposes: spiritual supremacy and physical domination over the society. Yet Muslim history also teaches that Islam is simultaneously capable of sectarian diversity and sectarian intolerance. While threats to public order and safety may, in appropriate cases, justify a limitation on the public expression of heretical religious views, "an Islamic regime or 'network' of any size or purpose that uses a religious rationale to silence its political enemies abuses both human rights and its Muslim cultural heritage" (Arzt 2002: 44; see also Künkler 2013).

The overall thrust of the Iranian Constitution and various laws is the primacy of measures that promote and protect the government, which is itself dominated by clerics of the Shiʿa Islamic tradition. This law-based effort to maintain control of all aspects of society has undercut the cause of religious freedom and means that even historical non-Shiʿi religious groups listed in Article 13 of the Constitution encounter many difficulties and considerable rancor as they practice their religion. Discrimination toward and maltreatment of members of historical religious minorities occurs in Iran, as is well documented by Tamadonfar and Lewis (2020), who discuss many problems experienced by the three approved minority religions listed in Article 13.

Contemporary Zoroastrians in Iran are a tiny population famous for keeping alive the ancient religion of Iranians' ancestors despite centuries of marginalization, discrimination, and persecution after the Islamization of the region (Stausberg 2012). After the majority of Iran's population converted to Islam as a consequence of the seventh-century Arab conquest of Persia, Zoroastrians grouped themselves in the Yazd and Kerman provinces, finding there "last bastions" to maintain their religion (Niechciał 2023). With minor exceptions, Zoroastrians, who had historically been relatively well treated in Iran, faced challenges under the Islamic Republic from the outset. During the Interim Government of Iran (4 February–6 November 1979), guerrillas walked into the main Tehran fire temple, removed the portrait of the Prophet Zoroaster, and replaced it with one of Ayatollah Khomeini (Fischer 2003: 229). Sayyid

[18] For instance, in two momentous statements by Ayatollah Khomeini, we read: "Islam is the religion of politics [*al-Islām dīn al-sīyāsa*] . . ., so whoever assumes that the religion is separate from politics is therefore ignorant, neither has known Islam nor politics" (2013, 1: 245) and "Islam is the government [*al-Islām huwa al-ḥukūma*]" (2009: 633). These expressions emphasize the idea of "unity and sameness of Islam and government" (Fazel Lankarani and Ghasemi 2022).

Ruhollah Khomeini, the architect of the Islamic Republic, dismissed Zoroastrianism as an "old and inveterate sect" and referred to Zoroastrians as "reactionary fire-worshippers," calling them by the derogatory term "gabr" (Foltz 2011: 77). But, interestingly, as a religious minority, Zoroastrians enjoy certain freedoms denied to the Muslim majority, including some leniency in holding social and community events free from heavy-handed governmental intrusion, and freedom to have closed events with mixed genders,[19] performing their religious rituals, and consuming alcohol.[20] Yet these freedoms are subject to local circumstances that govern communal relationships and general trends in governmental policies toward treatment of religious minorities.

In reference to Jews, those who voluntarily live in Iran have a special Iranian–Islamic identity and have been influenced by the mainstream culture (Hasannia, Fazeli, and Fazeli 2023). Though they usually lead a peaceful life alongside others and are socially recognized, they feel scrutinized by the government and the majority, which makes them feel marginalized. Thus they are careful in their relationships with others, behavior that is more prevalent among Jews than other minorities because their population is very small and they sense a need to be more cautious.

Anti-Zionism is today one of the most radical ideological pillars of Iran's regime (Menashri 2006; Rezaei 2019: 215–42), and antisemitism is one of its political byproducts and a manifestation of intense sentiments toward Israel. While it serves Iran's regional aspirations, antisemitism also constitutes an important component of the Islamic Republic's official ideology directed at both Iranian and foreign audiences.[21] This stems from failing to sufficiently

[19] For example, branch 39 of the Appellate Court of Tehran province, in decision No. 9109970223901448, dated 23 February 2013, acquitted two people belonging to religious minorities of "committing the *ḥarām* act of taking part in the mixed-gender party," arguing that "they are from religious minorities . . . and are only bound to observe their own religious criteria [and canon], in accordance with which there is no prohibition for them respecting participation in a mixed-gender party."

[20] When it comes to the *ḥadd* punishment for the crime of consumption of *muskir* (an intoxicant), non-Muslims are exempt from the law imposed on Muslims (i.e., they are not sentenced to flogging), provided they do not use *muskir* "publicly" or use in their "houses of worship" – for example, the synagogue and the church (Khomeini 2013, 2: 513). On this point, consider the judgment rendered by branch 1088 of the General Criminal Court of Tehran, upheld by branch 9 of the Appellate Court of Tehran province in decision No. 9209970220901290, dated 2 March 2014: "Christians are allowed household production and consumption of alcoholic drinks." However, "selling" alcoholic drinks by religious minorities is criminal (decision No. 9309972124200069, dated 5 April 2014, given by branch 1088 of the General Criminal Court of Tehran, upheld by branch 4 of the Appellate Court of Tehran province in decision No. 9309970220400273, dated 28 May 2014).

[21] Litvak (2020) argues that in view of the political situation in the Middle East, the ordinary Shiʿa consumer of religious or political literature is rarely exposed to any alternative attitudes toward Jews other than the dominant discourse. Several factors seem to facilitate broad acceptance of

differentiate the borderline between Jews and Judaism (the religious dimension) on the one hand and Zionists and Zionism (the political dimension) on the other. The two are often regarded as similar constructs in Iran, especially among the general population (Shahvar 2009; Jaspal 2015). Furthermore, "[a]bundant evidence traces Iranian anti-Semitism to Shiite Muslim ideology ... [T]he maintenance of Khomeini's overt anti-Semitic and anti-Zionist ideology may constitute a means of safeguarding the continuity principle amid important social and political change in Iran ... [T]he 'Jewish threat' to continuity is actively accentuated by the regime" (Jaspal 2013: 252; see also Litvak 2021: 73–111). Fox and Topor (2021) argue that antisemitism and discrimination are two distinct concepts. While antisemitism is a negative attitude toward Jews, discrimination is a negative real-world action taken against Jews. From this perspective, one can hold antisemitic beliefs but not discriminate, while another can discriminate against Jews but be less antisemitic in general. In this context, antisemitism is seen as a potential cause of discrimination against Jews, but not the only one. Fox and Topor also found that GRD against Jews is below average in Christian-majority countries, but societal discrimination is far higher than that most other religious minorities confront.[22] In Muslim-majority nations, most Jewish minorities are very small and societal-based religious discrimination (SRD), on average, is lower than SRD against Christians but higher than SRD against other religious minorities. However, they assessed the condition in Iran to the contrary, with GRD against Jews almost three times higher than SRD.

Faced with the constraints of international expectations and the pressure of Western public opinion sensitive to expressions of antisemitism, Iranian officials reject antisemitism as a Western phenomenon with no precedent in the history of the Islamic Republic. However, "Jews have been the subject of ... accusations, such as having a desire for world control, exaggerating the dimensions of the Holocaust, committing genocide, using blood in making unleavened bread, and distorting Holy Scriptures" (Shahvar 2009: 82; see also Litvak 2017). Moreover, hate crime has been reported against Jews in Iran, specifically several bombings of a synagogue (Nikookar and Hemmatpour 2012: 115).

anti-Jewish arguments: the widespread dissemination of such themes in mass media may serve as an indication of their popularity; the Israeli-Palestinian conflict and sympathy for the Palestinians promote popular readiness to believe hostile charges against Jews; the resort to themes that are deeply rooted in religious tradition makes such dissemination and absorption easier; and the linkage of the Jews with other enemies of Shiʿism – from the West to the Wahhabis – is used to justify a perception of Jews as a metaphor for evil and as an explanation for other threats. Those who are disillusioned by the Iranian government's official ideology may be less inclined to accept anti-Jewish propaganda, however.

[22] This is particularly interesting because Grim and Finke (2011) argue that SRD is a precursor to GRD, while Fox (2020) found that this is not always the case, and this pattern of relatively low GRD coupled with high SRD is unique to Jews among all religious minorities.

Bans on proselytizing and conversion away from Islam are among the most common forms of religious discrimination in the Islamdom (Fox 2016: 158). The Iranian Establishment is no exception and has shown a fierce preoccupation with non- and anti-Islamic religious propagation and the conversion of Iranian Muslim citizens to other faiths and regards this as a "national security threat" (Meral 2013). To this end, for instance, religious minority leaders are forced to prohibit Muslims from entering their religious sites and engaging in their religious rituals. Choksy (2012) claimed that several Zoroastrians and Muslim converts to this ancient faith were arrested in August 2011 and sentenced to public lashings plus many years in prison for ostensibly "propagating Zoroastrianism and organising ancient ceremonies." Further, significant restrictions are imposed on religious books, especially the Bible and any other books deemed to propagate and promote Christianity, which under the law may not be printed in or imported into Iran.[23]

Proselytizing and conversion come under regular public scrutiny, especially where conversionist/conversion-oriented movements are believed to be threatening to or disruptive of the social balance between majorities and minorities. Conversion primarily concerns the transformation of individuals and their identities (Paloutzian, Richardson, and Rambo 1999), but it also typically involves an important change in the membership in a community. Following Durkheim, Robertson contends that religion is constitutive of individual, diasporic, and transnational identity (2007: 23). Particularly, "religion has become a major vehicle for the expression of national identities" in the global era (Robertson 2009: 461). Hence, it would seem reasonable to assume a change of religious identity has important implications for national character. In this sense, conversions may be disruptive, especially when they occur systematically to certain social groups rather than apparently at random to individuals. Conversion is not just the experience of an isolated individual; it can involve the transformation of the status and identity of whole families and entire communities as well. For these reasons, the state may often quash proselytizing movements. Such conversionist movements threaten to disturb the balance of populations in societies that are diverse rather than homogeneous. Moreover, when proselytism is perceived to be associated with colonial powers, conversion can also be read as a cultural threat to an indigenous community. The response from a local community to such invasions can set off aggressive

[23] Even the possessor of such materials is at risk of prosecution. For example, in decision No. 86/4/19–409, dated 10 July 2007, branch 106 of the General Criminal Court of Hamedan found an Iranian citizen who was a follower of a minority faith guilty of "keeping *ḍāllih* [i.e., misguiding and perverse] books" and ordered their destruction (*maʿdūm-sāzī*) because it believed "the existence of the mentioned books is harmful to the society."

religious competition, resulting in violent civil conflict. Consequently, conversion is important socially and politically because changing individual allegiances almost inevitably changes social and political identities. Therefore, conversion movements often represent a challenge to the cultural definition of membership and the criteria of inclusion in society. This is particularly the case with Muslim-majority societies such as Iran, Pakistan, Afghanistan, Saudi Arabia, and Egypt, where religious affiliation is closely entangled with the definition of citizenship. "Religious faith" is indeed a double-edged sword that can either hinder or enhance someone's citizenship, as when state laws assign more rights and privileges to practitioners of some religions than to others (Nyhagen and Halsaa 2016: 114–52).

Despite defining "persecution on religious grounds" as a "crime against humanity" in Article 7(h) of the Rome Statute of the International Criminal Court, the global persecution of Christian minority communities occurs. Governments brandish different varieties of control efforts with different kinds of objectives, ranging from the annoyance and harassment of Christians to their outright extermination. The regimes in which persecution occurs are highly diverse – from Muslim-majority countries to brutal authoritarian regimes and failed states but also relatively stable and well-established electoral democracies such as India and Sri Lanka, whose very democratic structures incentivize groups to target Christian minorities in order to solidify the political support of non-Christian majorities (Philpott and Shah 2017).

At the time of the 1979 Revolution, there was no sizable community formed by converts from Islam to Christianity, but today Iran is home to a large number of Muslim-background Christians (MBCs). Notwithstanding some unrealistic statistics (e.g., Miller and Johnstone 2015), researchers estimate thousands of MBCs are in the country, most of whom have been recruited to Protestant evangelical denominations and Pentecostalism. These groups, although making up only a small percentage of the Christian population living in Iran, have been invariably treated harshly by Iranian authorities (Van Gorder 2018). Specifically, authorities have taken legal action against evangelical Christians who set up, lead and run, or simply take part in home churches and purportedly promote Zionist evangelical Christianity. For example, branch 26 of the Islamic Revolutionary Court of Tehran, in decision No. 26/35/96, dated 24 June 2017, sentenced four Christian converts to ten years of imprisonment for "acting against national security by the administration and establishment [*idārih wa tashkīl*] of the illegal house church and promotion of Zionist Christianity." Also, as a complementary punishment, the court sentenced two of them to be sent into exile for two years, one in Nik-Shahr and the other in Borazjan.[24] In another

[24] This verdict was upheld by branch 36 of the Appellate Court of Tehran province in decision No. 9609970223601689, dated 24 December 2017. However, the Supreme Court later overrode the ruling, ordering a retrial. The case was then sent before branch 54 of the Appellate Court of

case, branch 1 of the Islamic Revolutionary Court of Karaj, in decision No. 9709972664101098, dated 9 March 2019, convicted five Christian converts of "propaganda activity against the sacred *niẓām* of the Islamic Republic of Iran." One of the converts was condemned to fourteen months, taking into account recidivism rules, and the rest of the accused received four-month prison terms. In another case No. 9309980264001044, four Christian converts were deemed guilty by branch 2 of the Islamic Revolutionary Court of Isfahan of "propaganda against the *niẓām* of the Islamic Republic by organizing secret meetings, counter-revolutionary movements under the guise of Zionist Christianity, and communicating with Seven, Nejat, and Mohabbat satellite television channels [all affiliated with evangelical Christianity]" (decision No. 9309970367301107, dated 26 November 2014). The court sentenced one of them to one year and the others to nine months in prison. In another case, branch 26 of the Islamic Revolutionary Court of Tehran, in decision No. 26/34/97, dated 29 April 2018, sentenced a Christian convert to six months' imprisonment due to "membership in the unauthorized house church."

According to Philpott and Shah, the reasons motivating so many state and non-state entities to inflict different kinds of persecution on Christians are remarkably diverse:

> Perhaps the most common and widespread reason for Christian persecution – both in its more severe and in more mild forms – is the characteristic Christian insistence on being different and independent from comprehensive political control or cultural hegemony . . . Other factors vary across a wide range, some pertaining to genuine aspects of Christian theology and conduct, and others involving politicized and largely manufactured perceptions of Christian communities and their intentions. In numerous contexts outside the West, governments and majority religious communities perceive the very existence of a Christian minority as a pro-Western Trojan Horse . . . [S]ome groups and governments sincerely believe that Christians are agents of the West's strategic, political, religious, or cultural interests; others deliberately exaggerate and propagate this notion to advance their own political or religious agendas. (2018: 7–9)

On the strength of the "perceived threat" narrative, religious persecution is seen not as an act of belligerence but as a requisite means of legitimate political and cultural self-defense. This "necessity defense" is used to justify extreme actions against an enemy whose very existence is believed to constitute a danger. Partly because of long and painful histories of Western exploitation and colonial domination, in which Christianity often played a role, this narrative of the Christian "fifth column"

Tehran province. It reduced the jail sentence of two of the convicts to six years, one of them to two years (decision No. 9909970225800726, dated 16 June 2020), and one of them to three years (decision No. 9909970225802710, dated 8 February 2021).

enjoys significant resonance and influence in numerous contexts, particularly the Middle East and North Africa, as well as in South and Southeast Asia.

Other religious minorities do not have even the meager protections Article 13 of the Constitution allegedly offers (UN Doc. 2019: 10–18). For example, Bahaʾis are systematically discriminated against and deprived of some fundamental and citizenship rights, such as higher education and state-sector employment (Yazdani 2015).[25] Despite discrimination and repression, the state has paradoxically asserted: "[T]he situation of Baha'is in Iran is improving … Muslim Ulamas have declared Baha'ism as heresy. The centre of Baha'ism is located in Israel and is under the direct control of Zionism. Baha'is are enjoying the same rights as any other citizen in the Islamic Republic of Iran and no one is persecuted for being a Baha'i" (UN Doc. 1991b: 105).[26] They commonly face prosecution and punishment for the charge of *acting against the national security of the country* through such deeds as "propaganda against the *niẓām*," "establishing and/or organizing and running, or membership in illegal associations or groups," and "espionage," which are strongly assumed to be perpetrated in the interests and on behalf of foes, particularly the Zionist regime.[27]

Iranian courts have hitherto found a fair number of Bahaʾi believers guilty of various forms of conspiring against the *niẓām* and the established order. For example, branch 2 of the Islamic Revolutionary Court of Sari, in decision No. 9109971512600010, dated 3 April 2012, sentenced a Bahaʾi citizen to one year in prison under the charge of "propaganda against the *niẓām* by the propagation of the *ḍāllih* Bahaʾi cult."[28] In another case, branch 1 of the Islamic Revolutionary Court of Kashan, in decision No. 9109973659000330, dated 6 June 2021, condemned two Bahaʾi citizens to five months' imprisonment on the charge of "propaganda activity against the *niẓām* of the Islamic Republic of Iran (propaganda in favor of the cult of Bahaʾism)." Nevertheless, the court suspended the penalty for four years. In another case, the first branch of the

[25] Branch 16 of the first instance of the Administrative Justice Court of Iran (AJCI) stated in decision No. 9209970901600264, dated 7 May 2017: "Since the cult of Bahaʾism is not of the official religions mentioned in the Constitution, employing the Bahaʾis in a public-sector company and paying salaries, including insurance premiums [*ḥaqq-i bīmih*], is unconstitutional."

[26] Another example of such statements is: "Alongside the recognized religious minorities, the rights of all citizens – including the followers of the Bahaʾi sect – are respected" (Human Rights Council 2014: 20).

[27] On 10 April 2014, the then-first deputy of the judiciary of Iran, Sayyid Ebrahim Raisi, told reporters in Mashhad: "Although we do not recognize Bahaʾism as religion and, based on historical documents, we consider the Bahaʾi current to be a British-made current, the Bahaʾis who have been arrested and tried have been accused of spying for the Quds occupying regime" (IRNA 2014).

[28] Branch 10 of the Appeals Court of Mazandaran found the trial court's judgment "free from legal defects" and upheld it, but only commuted the appellant's incarceration to a fine of 40 million rials in favor of the state (decision No. 9209971516301592, dated 26 February 2014). To put it differently, the court of second instance upheld the decision, but reduced the severity of the penalty.

Islamic Revolutionary Court of Bushehr, in decision No. 9800106, dated 5 May 2019, convicted seven Baha'i citizens of "membership in the *ḍāllih* group and cult of Baha'ism with the intent to disrupt the country's security," and sentenced each of them to three years in prison, as well as a two-year *ne exeat republica* (i.e., the court barred them from leaving the country). Those convicted petitioned for appellate review, but branch 4 of the Court of Appeal of Bushehr province upheld the trial court's verdict and made an important remark: "The Baha'i cult is of the cults hostile [*mu'ānid*] to the *niẓām*, and the purpose of the said cult is to disturb the security of the country; hence, membership in it constitutes a criminal offense" (decision No. 9809977740401188, dated 17 November 2019). In another case, branch 1 of the Islamic Revolutionary Court of Semnan, in decision No. 9109972317300319, dated 16 August 2012, sentenced a Baha'i citizen to two years in prison for "formation of and membership in unlawful groups and committees [*hiy'at-hā*] affiliated with the Baha'ism establishment" and to one year in prison for "propaganda against the *niẓām* and in favor of the said cult," and also to the seizure of the discovered documents (such as Baha'i religious books and pamphlets) (the verdict was upheld by branch 4 of the Appeals Court of Semnan province by decision No. 9109972315401004, dated 20 November 2012). The crackdown on the Baha'i minority is officially explained by their supposed "wickedness and perilousness." Indeed, in the case of Baha'ism, the government of Iran has sought to fuse theology and politics with accusations of depravity and danger (Karlberg 2010). Exclusionary and extensive discriminatory practices against Baha'is and their predecessors are not limited to Iran – they also were persecuted in 1962 in Morocco, and their activities were banned in 1960 in Egypt and 1970 in Iraq (Sanasarian 2000: 53).

A 1993 document revealed the government had adopted a blueprint for the silent strangulation of the Baha'i community. The blueprint came in the shape of a memorandum on how to deal with "The Baha'i Question," which had been drawn up by the Supreme Council of the Cultural Revolution (SCCR) on 25 February 1991 (Bahá'í International Community 1993: 36–41). The memo came to the attention of the international community in 1993 via the UN Special Rapporteur's account. According to Reynaldo Galindo Pohl, the document was obtained as "reliable information" just as the annual report on Iran to the UN Commission on Human Rights was being completed (UN Doc. 1993: 55). The memorandum's central focus was that the Baha'is of Iran were treated in such a way that "their progress and development are blocked" and it revealed for the first time that the campaign against the Baha'i minority was centrally steered and directed by the government.

Of course, the anti-Baha'ism tradition predates 1979, at the governmental level as well as the level of social stigma and popular discrimination (Martin 1984;

Tavakoli-Targhi 2008; Yazdani 2011; Amini 2012, 2014; Vahman 2019).[29] Baha'ism traces its origin to 1844 in Iran as the millenarian movement of Babism, led by a young merchant, Sayyid ʿAli-Muhammad Shirazi (1819–1850), who took the title "the Bāb." He put forward claims until his death: he claimed to be the Gate (*Bāb*) to Imam Mahdi (pbuh), the messianic figure expected by the majority religion of Iran, Twelver Shiʿi Islam; to be Imam Mahdi himself; and, beyond this, to be an agent of the Divine and a messenger (*rasūl*) of God, the inaugurator of a new religious dispensation superseding and abrogating Islam and the Qur'an (Saiedi 2022). The Babi faith met opposition from its very beginning. Less than one year after the Bāb put forward his initial claim in May 1844, a combined panel of Sunni and Shiʿi *ʿulamā'* in a trial in Baghdad of the Bāb's emissary to Iraq unanimously condemned the Bāb as a heretic and apostate. By a majority, they sentenced his emissary to death for spreading the heresy (Momen 1982). The writings and actions of the Bāb were provocative, but nothing in them suggested an initiation of violence. Over a period of time, however, Shiʿite religious leaders escalated matters, calling on the state to halt the spread of the movement. This led eventually to violent confrontations in three locations of Iran in 1848–1850 (Momen 1983, 2018; Walbridge 1996; Zabihi-Moghaddam 2002). In 1850, Prime Minister Amir Kabir decided that the best way of putting an end to the Babi upheavals and insurrections was to execute the founder of the movement, who was being held in prison. The fatwas of two clerics who condemned the Bāb to death on the grounds of apostasy aided this idea as well (Amanat 2005: 394–403). At last, the Bāb was executed in Tabriz on 9 July 1850 (MacEoin 2009: 409–49).

Following the severe persecutions of the Babis in 1848–1850 and the execution of the Bāb, Babism was left shattered and with no clear leadership. In Tehran, two differing groups appeared among the Babis of the city. One group, under the leadership of Mullā Shaykh ʿAlī Turshīzī (known as ʿAẓīm) and Mirza Yahya Nuri (known as Ṣobḥ-i Azal), wanted to go to war with the Iranian state, partly to fulfill their apocalyptic and millennialist vision and partly out of revenge for the persecution they had suffered. The other, under the leadership of Bahā'u'llāh, looked to rebuild relationships with the government and advance the Babi cause by persuasion and the example of virtuous living. On 15 August 1852, a small, radicalized faction of the Babi community attempted to assassinate the monarch of Iran, Naser al-Din Shah Qajar (Momen 2008a). The attempt on the life of the shah failed and unleashed a nationwide general massacre of the Babis. Repercussions of the attempted assassination last to the

[29] Some claim that after the establishment of the Pahlavi regime, the Baha'is enjoyed legal rights like others, and many Baha'is could achieve prominent statuses (e.g., Khoshnood 2019). But other scholars have largely refuted such claims (see, e.g., Yazdani 2017).

present day. Although Bahā'u'llāh's policies were the opposite of those that inspired and fired up the attempted assassination, most Iranians knew the Baha'is as the Babis until well into the twentieth century, and the atmosphere of hatred and fear created by the attempted assassination was transferred to them. This enabled the clerical and cultural enemies of the Baha'is in Iran in subsequent generations to persecute them, target them by labeling, and implicate them in conspiracy theories.[30] The ultimate goal of these continuing efforts is to stigmatize and stir antipathy toward Baha'ism among the population.

Perceived betrayals and conspiracies of some Baha'is against Iran's national sovereignty have led the Islamist regime presiding over the country to lump all adherents of the group together, as though they are a single entity sharing communal guilt – "the sins of one being visited upon all." This has created an agenda aimed at obliterating and forcing Baha'ism out of existence.[31] This collective culpability approach has replaced individual liability, which relies on fundamental principles of modern criminal law, that of the presumption of innocence and individual criminal responsibility.[32] The tactics of suppression have always existed; however, the current pattern has changed from "a brutal and partly chaotic campaign in the aftermath of the 1979 Islamic Revolution to an institutionalized process with well-defined policies" (Zabihi-Moghaddam 2016: 124). Meanwhile, fatwas and opinions of the late leader and the current leader of Iran, as well as other senior conservative members of the clergy, have facilitated this campaign against the Baha'is (Bahá'í International Community 2023: 143–6; Khamenei 2023: 87–8; see also Yazdani 2012 and Sanyal 2019).

Meral briefly comments on the status of religious freedom in Iran, accounting for the repression of this internationally protected human right:

[30] Another notable case concerns the limited role of the Baha'is in the Constitutional Revolution of Iran (CR) (1905–1911) (Momen 2012; see also Momen 2008b). The Baha'is had a complex relationship with the constitutionalist movement, supporting the early stages of the CR. But they abstained from significant involvement in the later stages of the CR due to a number of factors, both internal ('Abdu'l-Bahā''s initial prohibition on taking part in public disorder or disruption and his later ban from all political involvement) and external (e.g., the opposition of the Shi'ite clerics and the creation of an antagonistic atmosphere by the Azalis). This withdrawal (or exclusion) of the Baha'is from the political process contributed to an atmosphere of fear, suspicion, and loathing toward them: the creation of an "enemy within." It is true that the position of the Baha'is drew on an already established scapegoating and othering of the Bābī movement even before the CR, but the establishment of the 1906 Persian Constitution gave this a legal basis as Baha'ism was not included.

[31] Pistor-Hatam points to Iran's treatment of the Baha'is as a bellwether trial in the court of public opinion: "The case of the Baha'i Faith clearly is the litmus test regarding the human rights of religious minorities in Iran" (2021: 219).

[32] This concept refers to the phenomenon of "blaming the collective or its members for a negative event caused by another member of the collective" (Manchi Chao, Zhang, and Chiu 2008: 730).

> Economic and political problems have posed a serious challenge to the regime's legitimacy, which continually seeks to maintain its rule and shift public attention away from its failures through imagined and actual conflicts with internal and external enemies. The current political unrest in the country has served only to escalate the need for scapegoats and to increase the number of arbitrary acts of the heavy handed rulers of the land, whose only remaining political legitimacy is the myth of being the guardians of the nation against its enemies. These two very temporal aims – socially engineering a complex society into a homogenized ideal, and creating mythic domestic enemies, who pose no actual threat and can therefore be harassed without fear of repercussions, in order to maintain state power – are the main reasons why Iran has come to perceive and respond to religious freedom as a national threat. In the rigid story of what the "Islamic" "Republic" of "Iran" ought to be and the supposed dangers against which Iranians have to fight . . . who breaks away from an officially sanctioned version of Islam will always find themselves portrayed as "enemies" and "moral deviants," no matter how faithful to the country they may actually be. (2013: 37)

Tamadonfar and Lewis argue that the systemic controls exercised over minority religions and even the three groups listed in Article 13 derive not from Islam directly but from an effort to exert control over Iranian society:

> To a large extent, the discriminatory practices against religious and sectarian minorities in Iran are rooted in the regime's belief in sectarian exclusivity and political self-interests, which have very little to do with the Islamic world view (2020: 1374) . . . In states dominated by a religious majority, there are always some violations of religious minority rights. However, as a significant departure from Iran's complex history of religious minority politics and rights, the Islamic Republic has built a legal and policy framework for systematic exclusion and intense discrimination. This strategy is neither appropriate nor is it necessary in view of the Islamic teachings on religious tolerance and accommodation. (2020: 1388–9)

These explanations can be reinforced by Sarkissian's (2015) argument, which maintains that, due to the costs of enforcement, politicians are unlikely to seek to regulate religion in the absence of political motivations. Aside from suppressing the potential oppositional capabilities of religious groups, governments may target specific religious groups because they threaten the identity or unity of a society. Maintaining control of Iranian society with its various minority religious and spiritual groups and currents, both approved and unapproved, as well as its politically oriented movements, is difficult and has contributed to governmental efforts to stifle nascent movements that develop. However, this is problematic given the apparent attitude changes of many citizens in post-Revolution Iran, as will be presented in Section 3.

3 Religious Life, Cultural Diffusion, and Religious Pluralism in Iran

The occurrence of the Islamic Revolution in Iran in 1979, followed by an extensive Islamization of society, resulted in unique developments concerning religious life in this theocracy. Since 2000, social scientists have engaged in lively debate on the nature of such developments and their implications for other Middle Eastern and Islamic communities. Kazemipur and Rezaei (2003) attempted to address this issue by relying on a rich set of empirical data gathered through a large-scale national survey of values and attitudes in Iran. The major finding of this research was that:

> The establishment of a theocratic regime in Iran has led to the transformation of the nature of faith, marked by a noticeable shift from "organized" to a more "personalized" religion, in which the emphasis is placed on beliefs rather than on practices. Also, among both beliefs and practices, more emphasis is placed on those with a purely individual nature, or with a social nature but organized through civic and nongovernmental bodies, as opposed to those commanded by the government. (2003: 347)

The analysis ends with a brief discussion of the implications of such developments for the debate among sociologists of religion concerning secularization and desecularization. Their findings indicate that any linear viewpoint on the demise or survival of religion in society will unreasonably brush aside the fact that religion is not merely a social institution, but also a "cultural resource" that individuals may draw upon, depending on their surrounding sociopolitical circumstances and their reading of those circumstances.

Hossein Godazgar (2020) offers a similar observation, claiming that dramatic shifts have occurred in the religiosity of Iranian citizens since the installation of the Islamic Republic. He discusses various historical and cultural developments that have resulted in the social construction of a much less dogmatic and more "spiritual" approach to Islam on the part of many Iranian citizens – for instance, the dramatic decline in participation in Friday prayers and related activities in Iran, among other things.

> Iranians have diversified the forms of their "religiosity" by creating and defining a variety of new venues and forms of "Islam" that are overall indicative of an individualized and semi-individualized "spiritualistic Islam" . . . [B]y "spiritualism" . . . I mean individualized, subjectivized and fragmentized definitions of "Islam" that, under the influence of societal conditions and global forces, are "socially constructed" in ways that go beyond the objective political and apolitical meanings defined by the institutionalized or organized Islam in the Iranian context: the "re-location of the sacred" from "institutionalized Islam" to "individualized Islam." (2020: 7)

He asserts that "'spiritualism' avoids and often loathes organized 'Islamism' or the political ideology of Islam" (7). Not only do "these forms . . . go beyond the requirements of an institutional Islam, such as the objective obedience of *Shari'a* and Shi'ite authority," Godazgar concludes, "but also dangerously oppose these requirements in some cases" (23).

Along with the shift in how Iranians experience Islam, Iran has witnessed the advent and burgeoning of "new spirituality" (*maʿnawīyat-girāyī-yi jadīd*) and new forms of religiosity, and many citizens have expressed an interest in a plethora of religious and spiritual ideas and philosophies.[33] This has prompted scholars to research why these phenomena have appeared in Iran and the rationales for some Iranian people's interest in and tendency toward them (see, e.g., Gholamizadeh Behbahani 2006, 2016; Talebi Darabi 2012; Talebi and Talebi Darabi 2013; Ramezani Tamijani 2016, 2020; Jaberian et al. 2017). An arena of unregulated religious and spiritual groups and currents now stands alongside the highly regulated, rigidly denominational religious market structured by the government. In the pluralistic religious and spiritual marketplace contemporary Iran has become, individuals become consumers of religious and spiritual "goods and services" and want to exercise a right to choose within a diversity of options, not exclusively what the government prefers.

Tellingly, Paul Heelas's description of the New Age movement in Europe and North America in the 1990s could also be applied to the terrain of Iranian alternative religions and spiritualities in the early 2000s:

> One's initial impression is of an eclectic hotch-potch of beliefs, practices, and ways of life. Esoteric or mystical Buddhism, Christianity, Hinduism, Islam, and Taoism enter the picture. So do elements from "pagan" teachings including Celtic, Druidic, Mayan, and Native American Indian. An exceedingly wide range of practices – Zen meditations, Wiccan rituals, enlightenment intensive seminars, management trainings, shamanic activities, wilderness events, spiritual therapies, forms of positive thinking – fall under the rubric. (1996: 1)

Iranian sociologist Sara Shariʿati Mazinani illustrates the validity of our claim about the cultural diffusion of religious and spiritual ideas from the West into contemporary Iran:

> From the seventies SH [1990s CE] onwards in Iran, we are facing not a movement, but training classes, meetings, and publications that are expanding. Formation of classes of self-knowledge, success, management of daily life, new therapies, etc.; the spread of sessions of Yoga, Zen, Meditation, etc.; the widespread publication of books and magazines in the fields of Buddhism,

[33] These have been variously called in Iran, more commonly referred to as "false mysticisms" (*ʿirfān-hā-yi nuw-ẓuhūr*), "emergent mysticisms" (*ʿirfān-hā-yi nuw-ẓuhūr*), and "deviant currents of thought" (*jaryān-hā-yi fikrī-yi inḥirāfī*).

> Hinduism, Osho, etc.; [all of] which originating from alternative medicine, depth psychology, and Eastern mysticism, all are the indications of the unprecedented and wide social reception of these phenomena. (2008: 11)

Dozens of NRMs and spiritual currents are present in Iran, including Sufism, Mysticism of the Ring/Cosmic Mysticism, Satanism, Yoga, Eckankar, the El-Yasin Community, the Baha'i Faith, Osho, Paulo Coelho, Technical Self-Meditation (TSM), Sai Baba, Dalai Lama, and New Thought, among many others (see Faʿʿālī 2010, 2022; Sharifi-doost 2020).[34] It appears that via modern means of communication, Iranian citizens have obtained information about many of the same ideas, movements, and groups that comprise the religious and mystical experiences of citizens of Western societies. Computer-based communication has enabled people to become familiar with a wide range of religious and spiritual beliefs and practices. Indeed, many of the new religions and alternative spiritualities have availed themselves of the opportunity to develop an internet presence. The prestige value of a web page is no doubt a contributory reason; however, more importantly, numerous religious organizations have realized internet surfers are using the internet to find ways to fulfill their spiritual needs. Even if surfers do not convert to the religions they find, they can learn of religious and spiritual beliefs and practices and savor something of them without having to seek out any organization.

The popularity of new religious and spiritual ideas in Iran should be understood within the context of considerable economic and sociocultural shifts in the years following the 1980s war with Iraq, which facilitated the rise of such alternative models in competition with traditional models of religion and spirituality. According to Doostdar, "economic and cultural liberalization enabled the rise of alternative spiritual models, on the one hand encouraging entrepreneurship, material ambition, and self-realization, and on the other hand lessening restrictions on publishing, such that a wide variety of mostly translated texts on spirituality (*maʿnaviyyat*) and mysticism (*ʿerfan*) could be printed and find a wide readership" (2018: 147).

Mohammad-Reza Anvāri (2012) offers a useful analysis of the stages of this growing interest in emergent religions and mysticisms and how the move toward newer religious and spiritual ideas has developed. His analysis reveals that the early period involved promoters of new ideas stressing that the ideas were not opposed to Islam but complemented it and that some of the new ideas meshed well with mystical tendencies within Islam. This first period lasted until about 1997 when a *reformist era* came into the open. Under the presidency of Sayyid Mohammad Khatami between 1997 and 2005, alternative religious and spiritual beliefs and practices (some of which had already circulated prior to the 1979

[34] TSM differs from Transcendental Meditation (TM), a form of silent meditation developed by Maharishi Mahesh Yogi (1918–2008).

Revolution) proliferated and were even promoted by some government officials. This was a time of lessening restrictions on publishing, with major efforts to translate many Western sources on various newer religious and spiritual phenomena. This resulted in a variety of mostly Western translated texts pertaining to religion and spirituality being printed and distributed within Iran.

For example, novelist Paulo Coelho's books have been well received within Iran, and his classic *The Alchemist* was translated in 1995 and has since been reprinted more than 100 times by different publishers in Iran. Coelho also visited Iran on 24 May 2000 and gave a number of public talks at a time when such activities were still allowed. Well-known Western works by Carlos Castaneda, Jiddu Krishnamurti, and others have also been translated and have had commercial success in Iran. One source claimed that more than 400 books dealing with yoga were published in Persian, most of them translated from Western sources (Behdasht Maʿnavi News Website 2019). More than 100 foreign writers in the area of New Thought have been translated into Persian. Hasanzadeh Tabatabaei (2019) studied the penetration of ideas of the New Thought movement into Iranian society. He writes about the availability of translated works of the prominent figures of this movement:

> Wayne Dyer with two million and seven hundred thousand copies, Catherine Ponder with one million and five hundred thousand copies, Florence Scovel Shinn with one million copies, Rhonda Byrne with one million copies, Louise Hay with one million copies, Jack Canfield with a physical presence in Iran and five hundred thousand copies, Debbie Ford with four hundred thousand copies, and Neale Donald Walsch with three hundred thousand copies, are the ones who have had the most published [translated] works in Persian. (2019: 113)

He concludes, "[T]he New Thought movement, with nearly eight million and five hundred thousand copies of written works in Persian, has been the most important and dangerous influential and newly emerging spiritual movement in Iran in the last two decades" (114).

However, a change of government occurred in the mid-2000s, when Mahmoud Ahmadinejad assumed the presidency. From this time on, new authorities were much less inclined to allow the importation of new religions and spiritualities into the culture. Indeed, people in positions of power and influence seemed to view this influx of Western ideas as part of an effort to undermine Iran's Islamic system of governance. Thus the wave of new mysticisms came to be viewed not as a scientifically interesting development but as a major threat to the state religion, the welfare of the nation, and the security and legitimacy of the government itself.

Henceforth, interest in alternative religions and philosophies was not so openly expressed by virtue of severe penalties that could be associated with anything construed as detrimental to the official ideological underpinning of the prevailing Islamic order. Research by Farshchi (2024) clearly demonstrates that governmental repression is a reality for NRMs in Iran. His study reveals that the level of repressing an NRM varied somewhat by the level of movement strength (operationalized in terms of membership size and geographic expanse), ideological origin (i.e., whether the movement is imported or indigenous and innovative), and the level of reaction to repressive measures against the movement. It also seemed that protests against repression of a given movement offer some limits to the repression experienced and reduce the severity of the state's actions against it. In Farshchi's analysis, a high level of strength for an NRM resulted in state repression, primarily through targeting the leader(s) with punitive actions, including short- and long-term incarceration and even capital punishment in some cases. For example, in decision No. 26/16/94, dated 26 July 2015, issued by branch 26 of the Islamic Revolutionary Court of Tehran, Mohammad-Ali Taheri, a so-called spiritual teacher and alternative medicine practitioner as well as the founder and leader of Mysticism of the Ring, was condemned to death for "spreading corruption on earth [*ifsād-i fī al-ʾarḍ*] by creating the cult of Cosmic Mysticism, and forming class[es], and expanding anti-religion and Shariʿa-contrary [*khalāf-i Sharʿ*] deviant thoughts, and unfounded claims, and weakening people's religious attitude and their religious beliefs in a wide and active manner at the domestic and foreign level." In a recent case No. 140168920006517965, a sixty-one-year-old citizen by the name of Saeed Khademi died on 6 November 2023 amidst trial in branch 29 of the Islamic Revolutionary Court of Tehran due to a heart attack. Hosein Askari Rad, the attorney who appeared for the deceased, attributed the death to the intense psychological stress and anxiety his client experienced in the courtroom (phone conversation with Sajjad Adeliyan Tous, 18 November 2023). Khademi was accused of "propagational and educational activity contrary to the holy Shariʿa of Islam" by practicing and instructing a form of Raja Yoga meditation known as Sahaj Marg.

As the reform period ended, concerns grew among Iranian religious authorities and conservative politicians about the rising interest in forms of religion and spirituality that were not approved and accepted by the state, and a number of critical publications on the newer religious and spiritual phenomena appeared correspondingly (e.g., Sharifi 2013; Mazaheri Seif 2016, 2020; Hamidieh 2020).[35] In one significant triggering event, on 25 February 2008, a special

[35] It is claimed that 245 books critical of newer religious phenomena were published by mid-2019, with 65 of them focusing on the growth of interest in Satanism (Behdasht Maʿnavi News Website 2019). Nevertheless, criticisms and accusations are not specific to emergent movements only, but

edition titled *Crooked Path* (*Kazhrāhih*) was made available to the public as a free supplement to the *Jam-e Jam* daily, a newspaper owned by the Islamic Republic of Iran Broadcasting (IRIB). This issue – a collection of critical reports, articles, interviews, and so on devoted to attacking so-called emergent quasi-religious and spiritual movements and currents – was distributed in a large circulation of 300,000 copies throughout Iran and contributed to an unfavorable attitude toward the groups and currents discussed therein. Another specific publication claiming to summarize Western efforts to control cults has been influential as well (Sharifiyan 2018), but this source is quite incomplete and misleading in its descriptions of alleged anticult activities in Western societies.

Many researchers and authors working in this area of study view these newer phenomena as a threat to officially sanctioned Islam. Their often theologically oriented writings argue forcefully for the control of so-called false mysticisms and support governmental efforts to limit such movements, groups, and currents of thought. In contrast, a few scholars have expressed concern about this approach. For example, Sadeghnia (2020) believes that the usual theological literature in Iran offers an incomplete and even erroneous approach, and that such phenomena are products of modernity and should be taken as social facts and explained sociologically rather than theologically. Saeedi (2022) describes two main stances toward NRMs in Iran. Some researchers and cultural practitioners see NRMs as a "superficial and fleeting phenomenon" that, due to the special circumstances of Iranian society, have been designed by foreign agents with "political aims and objectives" and in the direction of cultural destruction and societal collapse. These people usually recommend "physical and extreme solutions" to confront emergent mysticisms. Other commentators look on the new religious–spiritual developments as a "marginal counterculture and of little importance" in comparison with the surrounding dominant culture of the society. Saeedi criticizes the two positions:

> [I]n the present-time conditions of globalization and the expansion and intensification of communication in the world, new religious developments in Iranian society, beyond those two perceptions alluded to, are linked to religious and spiritual developments in the contemporary world. (2022: 163)

---

are also raised about long-established and traditional groups as well. Golestaneh touches on this issue with regard to Sufism: "As countless studies have shown, authority within Islamic communities is constantly negotiated, debated, and re-calibrated. This, of course, also includes authority within Sufi Orders, despite the naysayers – in Iran and elsewhere – who accuse Sufi leaders of demanding full and total obedience, of 'brain-washing' (*maghz-shooyi*) their followers in the most extreme cases" (2022: 20).

Of particular note are the writings of two leading lights of the Western anticult movement. Margaret Singer's *Cults in Our Midst* (2003) and Steven Hassan's *Releasing the Bonds* (2000) have been readily diffused in Iran and have become very prominent in official efforts to suppress newer religious and spiritual phenomena in Iran.[36] The book by Singer was translated in 2010[37] and the one by Hassan was translated in 2013.[38] Officials in Iran have accepted both as scientific treatments of cults in the Western world. Thousands of copies of the translations have been sold, and they have served as the major sources of many attacks launched by Iranian scholars and intelligence and security services.[39] Singer's "brainwashing" and Hassan's "mind control" notions espoused in their writings were prominent features of these treatments.[40] Singer's book has also been an inspiration for a few mass media films and serials dealing with so-called cults in Iran, some of which have been broadcast by national, government-run media outlets.[41]

In addition, two classic writings of British psychiatrist William Sargant (1907–1988) – *Battle for the Mind: A Physiology of Conversion and Brainwashing* (1957) and *The Mind Possessed: A Physiology of Possession, Mysticism and Faith Healing* (1973) – were translated into Persian in the 1990s and became available in Iran. The following books, among others, were translated in the twenty-first century: *Brainwashing: The Science of Thought Control* (2004) by Kathleen Taylor,[42] *Bounded Choice: True Believers and Charismatic*

[36] Release of these books in Iran might be considered a triggering event contributing to a major shift in policy and the eventual passage of anticult legislation discussed in the following section. If so, this clearly demonstrates that triggering events can be preplanned and manipulated to accomplish the goals of authorities who dominate Iranian society and politics.

[37] It was translated by Ebrahim Khodabandeh, a former member of the MEK, and published by the University of Isfahan Press in 3,000 copies (2nd printing, 2019, 1,000 copies). It was also reprinted by Nashr-i Māhrīs in 2019 in 1,000 copies (2nd printing, 2019, 300 copies; 3rd printing, 2020, 500 copies; 4th printing, 2020, 500 copies; 5th printing, 2020, 500 copies; 6th printing, 2021, 500 copies; 7th printing, 2021, 500 copies; 8th printing, 2022, 300 copies; 9th printing, 2022, 300 copies; 10th printing, 2023, 300 copies.

[38] This was translated by Ebrahim Khodabandeh as well, and published by Mu'assisih-yi Jām-i Jam in 3,000 copies.

[39] For an example of one publication that is mainly a rehash of Singer's major work, see Ahmadi and Shah-Hoseini (2017).

[40] For critiques of the pseudoscientific "brainwashing/mind control" terms, see, for example, Anthony (1999), Barker (1984), Richardson (1993b, 2014), Introvigne (2022), and Richardson and Adeliyan Tous (2023).

[41] For example, the TV series *The Soul Thief* (*Sāriq-i Rūḥ*), made in 2017 and aired on IRIB TV5, presented an evil, mysterious, and underground picture of NRMs, because of which the Ministry of Intelligence of Iran intended to battle against them.

[42] It was first translated by Saeed Sadr al-Ashrafi and published in 2021 by Nashr-i Gul-Ādhīn in 500 copies (2nd printing, 2021, 500 copies; 3rd printing, 2022, 500 copies). It was also translated by Salma Ahmadlou and Mohammad-Reza Bigdeli and published in 2023 by Markaz-i Taḥqīqāt-i Ṣidā wa Sīmā in 500 copies.

Cults (2004) by Janja Lalich,[43] *The Cult of Trump* (2020)[44] and *Combatting Cult Mind Control* (1988) by Steven Hassan,[45] *Cults Uncovered: True Stories of Mind Control and Murder* (2020) by Emily Thompson,[46] and *Dark Persuasion: A History of Brainwashing from Pavlov to Social Media* (2021) by Joel Dimsdale.[47] A few other books with more scholarly and balanced approaches have been translated as well, including: *New Religious Movements: Challenge and Response* (1999) edited by Bryan Wilson and Jamie Cresswell,[48] *Cults and New Religious Movements: A Reader* (2003) edited by Lorne Dawson,[49] *Controversial New Religions* (2005) edited by James Lewis and Jesper Petersen,[50] and *Encyclopedia of New Religious Movements* (2006) edited by Peter Clarke.[51] However, these have not received much attention in Iran.

One obvious conclusion to draw from all this is that Western influences have played a major role in the religious and spiritual life of many Iranians, as well as influencing governmental policies. Many religious and spiritual ideas and movements that have gained popularity in the West have permeated Iranian culture in spite of official efforts to limit such exposure. This was particularly the case during the reform era (*duwrān-i/duwrih-yi iṣlāḥāt*) discussed earlier in this Element. In addition, the availability of the internet in Iran has played a major role, as this has allowed ordinary citizens to access large amounts of information on emergent religious and spiritual groups and currents originated from inside and outside of Iranian society quite easily, and those interested in these newer phenomena can form internet-based groups to share their ideas with like-minded individuals. Moreover, hundreds of translated Western publications dealing with such phenomena have constituted a flood of material

[43] It was translated by Ali-Asghar Emdadi and published in 2021 by Intishārāt-i Ārīyābān in 300 copies (2nd printing, 2021, 100 copies).

[44] It was translated by Ali-Asghar Emdadi and Hamideh Gholipour and published in 2020 by Intishārāt-i Nigāh in 500 copies.

[45] It was translated by Sama Maʿsumizadeh and was published in two editions, one in 2022 by Intishārāt-i Wānīyā in 100 copies, and the other in 2023 by Nashr-i Dīrūz in 500 copies.

[46] It was translated by Yashar Mojtahedzadeh and published in 2021 by Intishārāt-i Sabzān in 500 copies.

[47] It was translated by Seyyed Ali Mousavi and published in 2022 by Intishārāt-i Nasl-i Ruwshan in 1,000 copies.

[48] Mohammad Gholipour was the first to translate this volume, published in 2008 by Nashr-i Marandīz in 2,200 copies. Also, it was translated by Mousa Akrami, which was further published in 2014 by Nashr-i Nigāh-i Muʿāṣir in 1,100 copies.

[49] It was translated by Kosar Taheri and Samaneh Gholami and published in 2018 by the University of Religions and Denominations Press in 1,000 copies.

[50] It was released in two volumes by the Research Center for Culture, Art and Communication. The first volume was translated by Zohreh Saeedi and published in 2016 in 100 copies (2nd printing, 2020, 500 copies), and the second volume was translated by Somayyeh Abdollahi and published in 2020 in 500 copies.

[51] It was translated by Hadi Vakili and published in 2021 by the Institute for Humanities and Cultural Studies in 300 copies.

promoting new religious and spiritual perspectives. Such materials have been well received by many Iranian citizens, as evidenced by sales of those translated publications. This is a sign of some Iranians' interest in such different approaches to life and spirituality.

But just as Western ideas about alternative religions and spiritualities have invaded Iranian cultural space, so there has been a concomitant diffusion of Western anticult perspectives on how to control and suppress these movements and currents, particularly after a change of government in 2005. Writings and concepts long debunked by scholars in Western societies (e.g., writings by Margaret Singer, Steven Hassan, and others cited in this section) have been selectively and strongly promoted inside Iran by government officials and those scholars and writers who are supportive of official state positions adopted in recent decades. Whether Western scholarly critiques of the works of major anticultists will eventually be acknowledged by Iranian scholars and officials is doubtful, however, given the high levels of concern about the attractiveness and spread of alternative religions and spiritualities in Iran.

4 Social Control of New Religious Movements in Iran: A Chronology and Analysis

Social control is a key concept in the lexicon of the modern social sciences, including sociology and legal studies.[52] This term famously refers to "the social processes by which the behaviour of individuals or groups is regulated" (Scott and Marshall 2009: 699) or "the mechanisms, in the form of patterns of pressure, through which society maintains social order and cohesion" (Carmichael 2012). Simply speaking, social control refers to purposive mechanisms used to regulate the conduct of people who are seen as aberrant, criminal, worrying, or troublesome. However, as the social world and its contextually grounded norms and values change over time, what is regarded as deviant or criminal behavior, belief, or characteristic may also differ from society to society, from one sector of society to another, from group to group, from one period of time to another, and from one social context to another.

Social control often manifests itself in a societal response employed by ordinary social actors against anyone counted as deviant, problematic, threatening, or undesirable. But it also sometimes appears as a governmental response exerted by state institutions (e.g., law enforcement agencies) in counteraction to perceived violations of norms and rules governing society. Both types involve the establishment and enforcement of behavioral

[52] See Black (1993) for a thorough discussion of law and social control.

standards for members of society for the sake of maintaining the social order and dealing with nonconformists to ensure law and order.

In this section, we expound on new efforts to pass significant anticult legislation in Iran, demonstrating the continued efforts by the cleric-dominated government to exert control over NRMs and spiritual currents. These efforts, which culminated in the passage of a new law in 2021 after several earlier attempts failed, maintained public focus on the perceived problem of unconventional religious and spiritual movements. These efforts were inspired and influenced by prominent Western anticult writings and by legislative efforts, particularly in France, a Western country with stringent anticult-oriented legislation.[53] This demonstrates that governmental restrictions on religion are often spatially clustered, not independent from other countries, and increases in a country's level of restrictions often reflect similar changes in other countries (Mataic 2018). Spatial clustering emerges through the diffusion of policies, where national governments mimic others' policies and practices, even when accounting for internal structural characteristics. While a country's internal structure is clearly a predictor of policies, today's world is a "global village" where national governments are not isolated from each other and where levels of restriction are susceptible to external influence.

Early Social Control Efforts by Iranian Authorities: 2005–2010

Contemporary efforts to control what are officially defined as "false mysticisms" and "deviant currents of thought" gained formal impetus with letter No. 2272–1/M, dated 22 February 2005, from the Office of the Supreme Leader of Iran.[54] This letter concerned the perceived problem of "the emergence and appearance [*burūz wa ẓuhūr*] of deviant individuals, organizations [*tashakkul-hā*], and associations under the cover of mystical and spiritual issues and the attraction of the country's youth to [and recruitment into] these organizations." This was the inceptive triggering event that drove the General Culture Council (GCC) to

---

[53] See Adeliyan Tous, Richardson, and Taghipour (2023) for a thorough discussion of France's anticult efforts to control new religious and spiritual phenomena.

[54] There were earlier efforts to control minority religions. For example, shortly after the 1979 Revolution, on 29 August 1981, the "Law on the Activities of Parties, Societies, and Political and Professional Associations, and Islamic Associations, or Recognized Religious Minorities" was passed, making clear that the government would exercise total control over all such activities. Further, on 12 January 1994, an enactment was issued by the 314th meeting of the SCCR regarding the "Legal Status of Various Sufi Orders" (*Jāygāh-i Qānūnī-yi Firqih-hā-yi Mukhtalif-i Sūfīyih*). The enactment made it obvious that, although Sufism could exist, it was to be limited in many activities. This regulation called upon the Ministry of Interior and other relevant agencies to "take careful attention that Sufi orders do not grow and develop," and also required the Ministry of Interior to "regard these cults as the society [*jam'īyat*] not as political parties, and to ask each of them to provide its details to the Ministry of Interior in advance in order to be given legal permission for religious activities in pursuant to the activity permit of the societies."

establish a committee on 1 March 2005 to investigate the phenomena of spiritual frauds, charlatans, and deviant subcultures promoting supposedly incorrect religious and spiritual doctrines and practices and manipulating the people.[55] The committee included representatives of law enforcement, the judiciary, the state-controlled mass media, several ministries within the state, and the Islamic Seminary of Qom,[56] among others.

The committee held eleven meetings during which it discussed developments in various spheres of life, including books, films, music, the press (*maṭbūʿāt*), the internet, and sports, all of which demonstrated the importance of cultural and ideological elements to developments in Iran. It then issued a three-part report, with the first section titled "Introduction" and the second section focused on "the causes and factors of the growth of deviant organizations and associations" active in the area of religion and spirituality.[57] This portion of the report identified, inter alia, "the legal vacuum and the unclearness of the limits and boundaries of the activities of these groups" as well as "the lack of coherence and coordination in expert and legal dealing with these organizations."

The third section offered "general and specific solutions" to the problems the committee reported in the second part. "Revising existing laws and setting [new] rules and regulations" were recommended to enable the judiciary and the intelligence and security apparatus to deal with norm-breaking activities of "*ḍāllih* cults." This report was passed in the 427th session of the GCC, dated 3 January 2006, and was sent to the SCCR for final passage afterward. On 14 November 2006, the SCCR approved the report in session No. 593, instructed the GCC's secretariat to pursue its implementation through "coordination with all relevant agencies" and to "submit the performance report of the relevant centers to the Supreme Council annually."[58]

On 18 November 2008, a proposal titled "Confronting the Emergence and Growth of Deviant Mysticisms" was introduced in the 494th session of the GCC.[59] Although the SCCR did not grant formal approval of this proposal, in practice many of its provisions were later sent to the entities named in the proposal

---

[55] The GCC is a subordinate institution of the SCCR, which was formed in 1985 for policymaking and directing the country's public culture. Its proposals do not have the force of law unless formally approved by the SCCR.

[56] It is the largest seminary in Iran, where Twelver Shiʿite clerics are trained. Many current Iranian political and judicial figures have been educated there. It is also an influential actor in the religious and cultural realms of Iran.

[57] *"Rāhkār-hā-yi Jilugīrī az Burūz wa Ẓuhūr-i Afrād, Tashakkul-hā wa Anjuman-hā-yi Inḥirāfī ba Pūshish-i Masāʾil-i ʿIrfānī wa Maʿnawī."*

[58] *"Ilzām-i Shuwrā-yi Farhang-i ʿUmūmī bi Piygīri-yi Rāhkār-hā-yi Jilugīrī az Burūz wa Ẓuhūr-i Afrād, Tashakkul-hā wa Anjuman-hā-yi Inḥirāfī ba Pūshish-i Masāʾil-i ʿIrfānī wa Maʿnawī."*

[59] *"Ṭarḥ-i Muqābilih bā Ẓuhūr, Burūz wa Rushd-i ʿIrfān-hā-yi Inḥirāfī."*

in the form of decrees and directives and put into effect by them. These entities included the Ministry of Education, National Youth Organization, Islamic Revolutionary Guard Corps, Center for the Management of the Islamic Seminary of Qom, and Supreme Leader's Representative Office in Universities, among a few others. The main tasks entrusted to those bodies could be summarized as follows:

- Training and organizing anticult/counter-cult experts, as well as supporting centers and institutions working in the fields of cultic studies and Islamic mysticism;
- Keeping religious minority groups under surveillance and not allowing them to openly and covertly propagate in universities;
- Raising public awareness about deviant cults and mystical currents and the diverse dimensions of their aberrant activities, such as recruitment methods, the dangers they pose, harms that can occur to members, and so forth;
- Preventing the promotion and spread of teachings of deviant cults and currents of thought through ways such as imposing a ban on printing (production) and publishing (dissemination) works concerned with such misleading movements and philosophies; and
- Carrying out research projects in order to obtain clear and realistic information on the extensiveness of deviant Eastern and Western mysticisms and their influence within Iranian society, causes of the tendency to embrace them, and so forth.

On 13 January 2009, the SCCR dispatched official letter No. 871/MDSh to the GCC concerning "the establishment of a study institute for cults and deviant currents" under the supervision of the country's cultural institutions. In response, the GCC in its 511th session, dated 25 August 2009, opposed the formation of the aforesaid center, declaring that both the Research Center for Culture, Art and Communication and the Research Institute for Islamic Culture and Thought should establish a specialized research group to investigate related matters that would contribute to combating cults and deviant groups within Iranian society.[60]

On 19 October 2010, in another important triggering event, Ayatollah Khamenei delivered a salient public address to the people of Qom in which he explicitly warned against the menace of anti-Islamic pseudoreligions and quasi-spiritual groups and currents in the country:

> You observe that since the 60s SH [1980s CE], from the blessed lifetime of the Imam [Khomeini], both foreign enemies and their mercenaries or unpaid servants from within [the country] have questioned and denied the religious sanctities, religious truths, and Islamic obvious facts [*bayyināt-i Islāmī*]. This has not been an accidental thing; they have relied on [and emphasized] this. This

[60] "*Tashkīl-i Gurūh-i Takhaṣṣuṣī-Pazhūhishī-yi Muqābilih bā Firqih-hā wa Jaryān-hā-yi Inḥirāfī.*"

> started from the incident of Salman Rushdie to anti-Islam Hollywood movies, to caricatures, to the Qur'an burning, to various events that took place against Islam in this corner and that corner [of the world], in order that they undermine people's faith in Islam and Islamic sanctities. *Inside the country, they have tried to shake the foundations of the religious faith of the people, especially the young generation, in different ways, ranging from diffusing debauchery and libertinism* [*ishā'ih-yi bī-bandubārī wa ibāḥī-garī*] [aiming to build a "permissive society"] *to promoting false mysticisms – fake form of genuine mysticism – to promoting Baha'ism, to promoting the network of home churches.* These are the things that are being done today with studying, planning, and prediction of the enemies of Islam. And its goal is to weaken religion in society. (italics added)

Ayatollah Khamenei also warned in a number of public speeches about deviant religious and spiritual currents and movements, all of which aid understanding the tangled mystery of repressing and curbing NRMs and spiritual currents in Iran in the post-Revolution epoch.[61] These addresses, which indicate the importance of the issue for Iranian officials, dramatically contributed to further assaults against minority religions and NRMs.

Efforts in 2013

On 10 April 2013, forty-four members of parliament (MPs) submitted the "Parliamentary Bill of Confronting Deviant Groups" to the Islamic Consultative Assembly (hereafter "the Parliament"). The preamble of the bill stated that:[62]

> These groups, both newly emerging and older, have one thing in common which is *deviant activities contrary to the holy Shari'a of Islam*, and therefore any proposed legislation that has intended to confront such phenomena must put this characteristic at the center of focus, and, at the same time, it must consider two essential issues as well. The first one is *avoiding attitudes of*

[61] For example, on 3 May 2008, he stated to academics and students in Shiraz: "Today, in your city and other places, . . . from contentless empty material mysticisms [*'irfān-hā-yi māddī-yi pūch-i bī-muḥtawā*] to obsolete religions, to organizations whose name is religion but is a political organization in nature, are trying and are struggling to decrease from and diminish this mass collection of Islamic force as much as they can" (https://farsi.khamenei.ir/speech-content?id=3431, accessed on 5 August 2023). On 9 October 2010, he said in a meeting with Hajj officials: "Different anti-Islamic, anti-spirituality, anti-truth cults have joined hands against Islam. They scrutinize to find the weak points and [mis]use those weak points, to find the infiltration points and strike us from those infiltration points" (https://farsi.khamenei.ir/speech-content?id=10241, accessed on 5 August 2023). On 11 October 2012, he told a meeting of teachers and professors of North Khorasan: "[B]e careful of these false mysticisms. These especially creep into universities. One of the plans [of the enemies] is that they infiltrate false mysticisms into the universities. This is one of the crippling things too. If someone is captured and affected by the unfounded and baseless claims of false mysticisms – which have also often infiltrated and entered from outside the country – it really cripples him/her" (https://farsi.khamenei.ir/speech-content?id=21153, accessed on 5 August 2023).

[62] "*Ṭarḥ-i Muqābilih bā Gurūh-hā-yi Inḥirāfī.*"

> *atheistic human rights contrary to the views of the Islamic thinkers*, particularly the Late Leader of the Revolution Imam Khomeini and the Supreme Leader [Ayatollah Khamenei]. (italics added)

This paragraph makes two pivotal points. First, in a theocratic state such as Iran, where all aspects of society (including legal, political, cultural, and social areas) are closely and in a totalistic manner monitored and regulated based on the Islamic-derived ideology of the regime, the governing body refuses to accept unreservedly religious pluralism by virtue of its policy of "religious intolerance" that advocates and cultivates "religious exclusivism." In such a climate, any religion or current of thought conflicting and dissenting with foundational tenets of national sovereignty faces severe governmental reactions. Indeed, a large body of literature strongly concurs with the risks of discrimination and persecution in cases of a strong state–religion entanglement. Fox, James, and Li refer to this as "state religious exclusivity," defined as "state support for a single religion to the exclusion of all others" (2009: 190). They recognize the religious exclusivity of Saudi Arabia and Iran as "extreme," noting in the case of Iran that it "supports a single version of Islam but tolerates some, but not all, other religions, which are given a second-class status" (190). Madeley (2003) argues that religiously exclusive states base at least part of their regime on non-pluralistic concepts, thereby increasing the likelihood that they will reject pluralism in other contexts. Endorsing one religion usually entails supporting it in some exclusive manner and doing so correlates highly with religious discrimination. To the extent that a state separates itself from support of a single religion, it would be expected to engage in less discrimination.

Second, in the 1970s, the Islamic Revolution movement in Iran rebelled against the dictatorship of the Pahlavi dynasty under Mohammad-Reza Shah (1919–1980), resulting in the replacement of a pro-Western authoritarian monarchy with an anti-Western authoritarian theocracy. Many Iranian clerical and academic figures began attacking universal norms of human rights, contending that the purportedly individualistic, secular, and Western orientation of human rights is alien to Islamic values and even anti-Islamic, and that the Universal Declaration of Human Rights (UDHR) and its progeny do not have their ideological origins in a common human quest.[63] These clerics and academicians also criticized one of the substantial theoretical foundations of the modern state,

[63] From the inception of the United Nations in 1945 there has been no consensus among Muslim states about whether Shariʿa precluded acceptance of principles of human, civil, and political rights because traditional interpretations of Islamic jurists have been difficult to reconcile with ideas such as full equality for men and women, bans on discrimination based on religion, and religious freedom.

secularism, as historically associated with despotism, dictatorship, and human rights abuses in the postcolonial era (Hashemi 2014: 445). Indeed, the Muslim experience defines secularism as an alien repressive ideology imposed first by invaders and colonialists and then perpetuated by postcolonial ruling elites. The perceived aim of such postcolonial efforts in the Muslim world, especially Iran, has been to eliminate the authority of the Islamic tradition.

Exemplifying these points, on 7 December 1984, Iran's former ambassador to the UN, Saeed Rajaee Khorasani, in a rare moment of unguarded candor, stated that post-Revolution Iran was not bound to comply with human rights. In remarks that Iran's human rights policy critics often cite, he proclaimed that the Islamic Republic would have no qualms about violating human rights if the official religion of Iran demanded it. According to the paraphrased record of his speech:

> [C]onventions, declarations and resolutions or decisions of international organizations, which were contrary to Islam, had no validity in the Islamic Republic of Iran ... The Universal Declaration of Human Rights, which represented secular understanding of the Judeo-Christian tradition, could not be implemented by Muslims, and did not accord with the system of values recognized by the Islamic Republic of Iran. His country would therefore not hesitate to violate its provisions, since it had to choose between violating the divine law of the country and violating secular convention. (UN Doc. 1984: 20)

According to Rajaee Khorasani, then, Iran's conduct was not to be measured by international human rights standards. The new normative standards were to be those of Islamic law, which might conflict with the Western-dominated international system – a system with values deriving from an alien, non-Islamic tradition. Actually, Rajaee Khorasani was unconsciously implying that, because of their religion, Muslims had rights inferior to those of Jews and Christians and thus could not claim the same standards of rights and protections under international law. Along with repudiating human rights law, he offered secular and non-Muslim states advice to the effect that nations that "could not live up to the divine standards of Islam should at least meet the minimum requirements established by international organizations" (UN Doc. 1984: 20). To his mind, Islam did, in fact, protect human rights but in consonance with its own values. And since these values were rooted in divine law, they were superior to those based on secular authority.[64]

[64] The following report to the Human Rights Committee exemplifies the juridical implications of this theological premise: "[The representative of Iran] stressed that the criteria for determining the validity of any law would be the values given by God and transmitted to earth, that since human traits were considered to be in harmony with revealed values, values derived from human civilization and from reason were held to be close to Islamic values, and that whenever divine law conflicted with man-made law, divine law would prevail" (UN Doc. 1982: 72).

In the analysis of Khorasani's remarks, Mayer observed:

> Obviously, Raja'i Khorasani's alternating presentations of "Islam" as the justification for the regime's violations of human rights and "Islam" as the guarantor of a higher standard of rights than what was afforded by international law were contradictory. The contradictions were necessitated by the regime's reliance on Islam as a legitimating device. On the one hand, the Islamic Republic needed a rubric like "Islam" to justify the long record of rights violations that it had already accumulated during its first years in power and that had provoked strong criticism. On the other, the regime's sole basis of legitimacy was Islam, and the more this Islam was associated in people's minds with rights violations, the less popular and credible – hence, less useful as a means of claiming legitimacy – it would become. (1996: 271)

The Islamic Republic, of course, was not eager to be identified with the position implicit in Rajaee Khorasani's stance, namely that Muslims could only claim an inferior standard as regards rights protections. Such a notion was embarrassingly akin to the colonialist paradigm of superior rights for Westerners vis-à-vis subjugated Muslim communities.

On that account, the Iranian government does not recognize human rights (such as the right to FoRB) in the same way as enshrined and defined in international instruments; rather, it rejects each provision of those supposedly atheistic documents if discerned as incompatible with Islamic rules and standards. The recognition of the right to change religion and the punishment of apostasy is exemplary here as perhaps the most controversial and intractable *perceived* conflict between human rights and Islam (Sachedina 2009).[65] Focusing on the drafting and adoption of the UDHR in 1948, Gunn (2020) evaluates whether a significant values divide exists between the Muslim and Arab worlds on one hand and the human rights regime on the other. He finds no inconsistencies between the values of the UDHR and Islamic law:

> [I]t appears that the real issue for Muslim critics of the UDHR is not that it interferes with the ability of Muslims to practice their religion, but that *it interferes with their wish* (which has no basis in traditional Islamic law) *to enlist the modern state* to compel compliance with religious law. Indeed, we might be so bold as to argue that there is a Quranic injunction against the state, or any earthly power, from using force to coerce compliance with religion: "there is no compulsion in religion." (2020: 161, italics in original).

[65] Explaining the historical background of this, Nowak writes: "Whereas many delegates in the HRComm and the GA were of the opinion that a right to change religion was an indispensable component of freedom of religion, this right was especially opposed by Islamic States, which feared that this might encourage proselytizing, missionary, and atheistic activities" (2005: 410).

Therefore, the problem is not an underlying conflict between the norms of the modern human rights regime and Islamic doctrines and rules, but the mistaken assumption that the modern nation–state is the proper institution that should be empowered, entrusted, or required to enforce its interpretation of Islamic law. Experience shows that the mixing of Islam and the modern state has trapped its citizens in concentric, hermeneutic mazes.

> Consider the case of Iran in 2000, where at least three official visions of Islam are locking horns within the regime over the future of the Islamic state, at the same time that they clash with equally authentic readings of Islam outside the ruling circles . . . All these Islamic (political) positions are capable of shifting, depending on who is in power and who is the main adversary in the struggle for power at any moment. What may remain fixed is religious rationalization for these positions. (Afshari 2011: 300–1)

The 2013 draft law contained a single article accompanied by two notes. The proposal was somewhat unfocused and cast a wide net that included everything from religions coming from China and India, atheism, Satanism, and others, to alleged Islamic-based groups viewed as unaligned with *true* Islam. The offenses introduced by the proposed law were misdeeds and wrongdoings associated with the creation of or belonging to such so-called deviant groups and currents and attempting to spread their ideas. It was assumed that combating the threats and dangers of cults should not be limited to harm and damage allegedly done after the fact, but such groups should be dealt with preemptively. The article started as such: "Whoever under any title practices Satanism, emergent mysticisms or other deviant activities contrary to the holy Shariʿa of Islam, if he/she is not subject to the *ḥadd* penalty, he/she shall be condemned as follows." The bill then listed a number of specific acts that would be criminalized with heavy lashes and jail sentences applied. Included were the sentence of "more than five to ten years of imprisonment or 31–74 lashes" against "whoever forms or administrates an organization, association, cult, institute, or society with more than two people in or outside the country" (subsection [a]); the punishment of "more than two to five years prison term and/or 31–74 lashes in case of propagational activity in real or cyberspace" (subsection [b]); and the penalty of "more than six months to a two-year imprisonment or 31–74 lashes" for "membership in or continuously attending meetings of" the entities outlined and set forth in subsection (a), which were taken to be deviant and problematic unless the person's ignorance of the corrupt goals and activities of such entities is substantiated (subsection [c]).

Apart from failing to observe the "principle of proportionality of criminal offenses and penalties," *ambiguity* in the proposed law was also objectionable. For example, the article criminalized any so-called deviant activity contrary to the Shariʿa in cases of relatedness to and falling under the rubric of the mentioned subsections, but did not specify what the instances of the said criterion might be. Such vagueness breaches a central rule-of-law requirement, the principle of legal certainty: law must be formulated with adequate precision and clarity so that those subject to it might foresee the consequences a given action would entail and be able to modify their behavior in order to protect against the arbitrary exercise of state power.

The Parliament Research Center adjudged the proposed bill to be "comprehensive and complete," in spite of some perceived minor defects. However, the Parliament's Judicial and Legal Commission remained silent, a position that can seem to be construed as a rejection. Why the proposal was left hanging is not obvious, but, for whatever reason, this proposal died.

Efforts in 2015

Another proposal, the "Parliamentary Bill of Prohibition against Formation, Propagation, and Membership in Cults," was unveiled on 28 December 2014 and signed by sixteen MPs when put forward to the Parliament.[66] According to the representative who mooted the bill, cleric Ahmad Salek Kashani, this proposal was necessary for several reasons, including some young people's proclivity for deviant currents and their alienation of their family and Islamic culture and society, as well as menaces of cults like Ahl-e Haqq, which is active in Kermanshah; Bahai'sm, which he viewed as "the spy service of Zionism" in Iran; and newly emerging mysticisms. He added that tackling cults such as Satanism is not just limited to Iran, but other countries have taken countermeasures on this matter as well. Moreover, these emerging mysticisms are Western countries' and antagonists' imports into Iran, by which they intend to weaken the Islamic culture and thought (phone conversation with Sajjad Adeliyan Tous, 12 June 2023). The opening page of the bill included this statement:

> Attempts have been made in preparing this draft law that deviant actions of cults – which are contrary to freedom and dignity, human identity and honor, public morals and order, and, most importantly, the security of the country – be considered taking into account Articles 12 and 13 of the Constitution and other codified laws of the Islamic Republic of Iran as well as the rules of international human rights.

This introductory section, dedicated to the "justificatory reasons" for presenting the bill, specifically cited Article 18(3) of the ICCPR, which lays the groundwork for imposing limitations on expressions of FoRB. This citation revealed

[66] "*Ṭarḥ-i Manʿ-i Tashkīl wa Tablīgh wa ʿUḍwīyat dar Firqih-hā.*"

that the national legislature was attempting to rationalize the "criminalization of religious freedom" by human rights standards in order to avoid condemnation from human rights monitoring bodies. Thus an international ideological standard was used in a counterintuitive manner to undergird what the political structure of Iran wanted to accomplish.

The draft of the bill consisted of three articles designed to combat cults and deter their manipulation and undue influence by filling the perceived legislative lacuna existing in the arsenal of criminal legislation, thus mending the realized *non liquet*. The draft law was derivative, inspired by and in part a literal translation taken from Western anticult materials. The impetus for the bill, discussed in Article 1, was "safeguarding humans against brainwashing, heterodox tendencies, ideological induction, deceptive conversion, and the creation of *wahn* [i.e., weakness] and *fitnih-yi iʿtiqādī* [i.e., chaos in and confusion about religious beliefs, which can lead people intellectually astray], as well as preventing deviant individuals', cults', and currents of thoughts' abuse." Article 2 penalized any person who "establishes" and "recruits" to and "administers" a cult whose purpose is "brainwashing, rocking the foundations of the religions [*ījād-i wahn dar mabānī-yi adyān*] and *fitnih-yi iʿtiqādī*." Note (1) of Article 2 specified twenty-one examples of the instances of weakening the foundations of the (recognized) religions and *fitnih-yi iʿtiqādī*, including:

- Identity stripping from deceitfully recruited (brainwashed) members;
- False claims in the religious domain, such as unfounded claim of communication with the prophets (pbut), Twelve Infallible Imams (*Aʾimmih-yi Aṭhār*) (pbut), the special deputies of Imam Mahdi, and so on;
- Acts of terrorism or destructive activities;
- Sexual, physical, or financial exploitation of individuals;
- Damaging an individual's decision-making power and persuading him/her to violate the rights of others;
- Compelling individuals (such as women and children) to receive specific pieces of training or encouraging them to adopt a specific lifestyle in order to allow mind control and/or psychological manipulation, thereby achieving dominance over them; and
- Exerting psychological and/or behavioral pressure and obtaining confession in different ways so as to control members.

The bill's drafters apparently had accepted the underlying assumption that "brainwashing" (and related concepts) can produce ideological and behavioral changes in a fully conscious, mentally intact individual. Note (5) of Article 2 obligated the Ministry of Intelligence to monitor crimes of cults and deviant currents of thought and to report offenders to the judiciary. Article 3 of the bill was dedicated to rules for confiscating all movable and immovable properties of cults and deviant currents of thought in favor of the government.

As with the 2013 proposal, there was ambiguity in the provisions of this bill. For example, terms such as *brainwashing*, *induction*, *heterodoxy*, and *mind control*, for which no explicit definitions were offered, made it difficult to understand the proposed law.[67] Because of serious flaws in the draft of the bill, and the perceived need to criminalize cults and cultism and the connected matters, efforts were made to develop a more acceptable alternative. On 20 May 2015, the Parliament Research Center released its evaluation of this bill, titled "Expert Comment on the Parliamentary Bill of Prohibition against Formation, Propagation, and Membership in Cults," which included a revised draft law.[68] The Research Center claimed that this proposed draft law was free from the flaws of the initial 2015 bill. However, the new draft law was not immediately considered and several years passed before it was formally submitted to and addressed by the Iranian legislature.

Efforts in 2018–2021

As discussed, there has been a growing perception within the authoritarian Iranian government that the increasing interest in emergent religions and alternative spiritualities has to be addressed forcefully. This led directly to efforts in 2013 and 2015 to develop legislation that would support more control over such phenomena. While these earlier efforts were not successful, eventually the Parliament addressed this issue once more. On 25 December 2018, the Parliament tabled for the third time another draft law, which was originally the same draft law the Parliament Research Center had offered on 20 May 2015, albeit with slight modifications. This persistence in handling such

[67] For instance, the definition of brainwashing given in the bill was: "Mind control, manipulating individuals' minds, psychological dominance over individuals, constructing the intellectual ideology of violation of human dignity and identity, deviance and thought reform, induction [*ilqā'garī*] and deceptive conversion, and specific ideological induction." When I [Adeliyan Tous] asked Salek Kashani, "Whence did such wordings and terms come? Did you use Western sources on cults and brainwashing/mind control when drafting the bill?" he gainsaid this hypothesis: "We had seen various sources, but the draft law was not a derivation from them." He was a firm proponent of mind control, believing it to be real. When I told him that many scholars have denounced and demolished these theses, he assertively replied that some qur'anic (e.g., Q al-Mujādila 58:19, '*Istaḥwadha 'alayhim al-shayṭān*,' i.e., Satan has overpowered and gained mastery over them) and hadith evidence implies mind control, and only modern language was used in drawing the draft law – serving up "old wine in new bottles." This is why such phrasings and the usage of such terms are seen in this document. He added, "Brainwashing, mind control, and the like are the enemy's cognitive warfare tools and have the scientific basis in cognitive science" (phone conversation with Sajjad Adeliyan Tous, 12 June 2023).

[68] "*Iẓhār-i Naẓar-i Kārshināsī darbārih-yi: 'Ṭarḥ-i Man'-i Tashkīl wa Tablīgh wa 'Uḍwīyat dar Firqih-hā.'*"

a controversial measure is itself a sign of how strongly some elements of the Iranian government felt about nontraditional religious groups.

The proposal's title was the "Parliamentary Bill of Adding Two Articles to the Islamic Penal Code," and sixty MPs had signed it at the time of submission.[69] Due to the relative similarity of the title and content of this bill to two other bills,[70] the Judicial and Legal Commission of the Parliament merged all three draft laws and named the new document the "Parliamentary Bill of Adding Two Articles to the Fifth Book of the Islamic Penal Code (*Taʿzīrāt* and Deterrent Punishments)."[71] The Judicial and Legal Commission consented to this new proposal on 25 February 2020, and it was put to the vote on 19 May in the Parliament Chamber, unanimously winning enactment. Ensuring compatibility of the legislation passed by the Parliament with the criteria of "Islam" and "the Constitution" required that the measure be submitted to the Guardian Council (GC) for inspection.[72] On 1 June, the GC returned the approved bill to the Parliament with a number of objections primarily relating to the ambiguities of terms and definitions. The Parliament then implemented a series of amendments to address the GC's objections and sent it back for the GC's approval on 1 November. The GC rejected the revised version once again and sent it back to the Parliament on 28 November, seeking more clarifications. On 13 January 2021, the Parliament for the second time, responding to the objections raised by the GC, made necessary amendments and awaited final approval. In the end, after several reviews of the Act of Parliament, the GC assented to it on 3 February 2021. On 15 February, Speaker of the Parliament Mohammad-Bagher Ghalibaf presented the Act to the president of Iran, Hassan Rouhani, and the president forwarded it to the judiciary and the Ministry of Justice on 17 February. The Act, nominated as the "Law of Adding Two Articles to the Fifth Book of the Islamic Penal Code (*Taʿzīrāt* and Deterrent

69 "*Ṭarḥ-i Ilḥāq-i Du Māddih bi Qānūn-i Mujāzāt-i Islāmī*."

70 The "Parliamentary Bill of Adding Articles to the Fifth Book of the Islamic Penal Code (*Taʿzīrāt* and Deterrent Punishments) regarding Insulting Legally-Recognized Religions and *Madhāhib* and Iranian Ethnicities" (*Ṭarḥ-i Ilḥāq-i Mawāddī bi Kitāb-i Panjum-i Qānūn-i Mujāzāt-i Islāmī (Taʿzīrāt wa Mujāzāt-ha-yi Bāzdārandih) dar Khuṣūṣ-i Ihānat bi Adyān wa Madhāhib-i Qānūnī wa Aqwām-i Īrānī*) dated 19 December 2018; and the "Parliamentary Bill of Fighting Racial Discrimination and Ethnic and Religious Hatred" (*Ṭarḥ-i Mubārizih ba Tabʿīḍ-i Nizhādī, Tanaffur-i Quwmī wa Madhhabī*) dated 2 December 2018.

71 "*Ṭarḥ-i Ilḥāq-i Du Māddih bi Kitāb-i Panjum-i Qānūn-i Mujāzāt-i Islāmī (Taʿzīrāt wa Mujāzāt-ha-yi Bāzdārandih).*"

72 The "Shariʿa guarantee clause" (SGC) is often found in authoritarian or imperfectly democratic constitutions (Lombardi 2013). Unsurprisingly, the designers of SGC enforcement schemes in nondemocratic or autocratic countries have generally tried to ensure that their SGC can be interpreted and applied in a way that permits or even promotes nondemocratic policies. Designers of authoritarian Islamic constitutions have thus been careful to vest the power of SGC enforcement in an institution little inclined to protect liberal rights.

Punishments)," was then promulgated on 22 February by publication in the *Official Gazette of the Islamic Republic of Iran*, a paper under the auspices of the judiciary, to become effective.[73]

Thus, after many attempts, a law was finally enacted to fight the perceived menace of new and deviant religions and spiritualities. The passage of the law clearly demonstrated that cultural, social, ideological, and religious factors can overwhelm other considerations when trying to address major contradictions in how Iranian society functions in respect of religion. Now we will offer some theoretical considerations on why passage took so long.

5 Conclusions, Relevant Sociological Theories, and Theoretical Applications

In Iran, ecclesiastical power is inseparably linked with state power and is foundational to its structure. This fact leads to the exercise of total control through legislation and legal processes based on the officially defined norms of the dominant religion, namely Shiʿism. Thus contemporary Iran demonstrates the concept of a thoroughly theocratic state with a supreme leader who exercises almost total control over governmental actions. The situation in Iran contradicts the idea of a "constitutional theocracy," where a government exercises control over religious impulses and movements by incorporating them into the governmental structure and using the judicial system to manage them (Hirschl 2010, 2012).[74] Hirschl briefly discusses Iran in his treatise, but his cursory treatment seems off the mark, especially in light of more recent events discussed herein. There seems little doubt that Iran is now an example of a *pure* theocracy totally dominated by one particular version of Islam.

---

[73] "*Qānūn-i Ilḥāq-i Du Māddih bi Kitāb-i Panjum-i Qānūn-i Mujāzāt-i Islāmī (Taʿzīrāt wa Mujāzāt-ha-yi Bāzdārandih)*." Persian text of the Act may be found at https://rc.majlis.ir/fa/law/show/1643402 (accessed on 21 March 2024).

[74] According to this theory, the constitutional establishment and enshrinement of religion is not only an ideational or a regime legitimacy-enhancing move, but also, counterintuitively, a rational, prudent strategy that allows opponents of theocratic governance to appear religiously committed without having to actually adopt theocracy's unappealing elements. Constitutional law and courts, as symbols of state sovereignty and authority, owe their existence to the body politic, not to a divine authority. They share an inherent antipathy toward rival interpretive hierarchies. Many of the jurisdictional, enforcement, cooptation, and access-to-power advantages that gave religious legal regimes an edge in the premodern era are now aiding the modern state and its laws in its effort to contain religion. Turning to constitutional law and courts to bring religiosity in check or to defuse its potentially radical edge is a rational choice of action by secularists and moderates. In spite of occasional and inevitable setbacks, it seems a prudent, judicious gamble. The "constitutional" in a constitutional theocracy thus fulfills the same restricting function it carries out in a constitutional democracy: it brings theocratic governance in check and assigns to state-controlled constitutional law and courts the task of building a bulwark against the threat of radical religion.

Given this conclusion, it seems strange that earlier efforts to legislate against alternative religions and new spiritualities foundered repeatedly before finally succeeding. One view is that this area may not have been as high a priority as some thought. However, continual discussions of these matters in official high-level governmental bodies were keeping the issue very much alive in public discourse. Mass-media coverage of the topic in Iran's controlled media market reminded members of the public that this is a sensitive area, and that government officials and clerics in charge of the Iranian government do not view participation in NRMs positively. Another view is that the passage of specific legislation in this area could lead to consequences that would be viewed negatively by some in the government of Iran. Such stringent laws could draw the attention and ire of human rights advocates and organizations that value human rights and religious freedom, thus calling critical attention to Iranian society. Additionally, given the religious diversity in Iran and the changing religious views of many Iranian citizens, perhaps government officials delayed passing legislation because it might cause social unrest.

Along the same lines, the draft laws were written and debated by different parliaments with different majority constellations that held divergent views on how much religion should be regulated and in which direction (some favored more *wilāyatī/wilāyī* and *revolutionary* tendencies, while others rejected these and yet others rejected further infringing regulation altogether). Moreover, this is the typical legislative process in Iran, where other far more important and far-reaching pieces of legislation have taken even longer.[75]

It is worth noting that, even as new legislation was being considered, mistreatment of members and leaders of NRMs and minority faiths was proceeding apace in Iran, as described earlier in this Element, despite the delays in approving a new statute to deal with the perceived problem of unauthorized religious groups and spiritualities. From the dominant religious community's point of view, all the representative groups of a particular other tradition may be defined as *outsiders* (in Becker's 2018 term). In particular, the Baha'is are seen as enemies of the Iranian government and are regularly persecuted for practicing their faith (Yazdani 2018). They are systematically discriminated against in many areas of

[75] In response to the question of why the legislative delays, Mousa Ghazanfar-Abadi, chairman of the Judicial and Legal Commission of the eleventh term of the Parliament, said the Commission classifies and addresses bills based on their "importance and priority," and the earlier two bills of 2013 and 2015 were possibly not urgent. He added, "we have (parliamentary) bills in hand from previous terms of the Parliament right now, and even from the seventh Parliament (27 May 2004–26 May 2008) such as the Trade Bill, which is still under review and discussion in the Commission" (phone conversation with Sajjad Adeliyan Tous, 11 June 2023).

life (jobs, property ownership, access to higher education, and other areas), and even in death, as Iran offers no approved cemeteries for the Baha'is.[76] And practitioners of other minority faiths, including even the three with some protections listed in Article 13 of the Constitution, are often dealt with quite harshly by authorities in contemporary Iran. The Iranian Constitution, as currently interpreted, and other existing laws have evidently institutionalized religious discrimination (Milani 2016). The jurisprudential and legal framework within which religious and spiritual communities are sharply restrained and their rights violated is directly linked to the state's principal objective of maintaining a national identity as an "Islamic" Republic.[77] Thus there has been little, if any, counter to directives derived from the dominant clerical Islamic ideology the Iranian regime has put in place. Nevertheless, as British sociologist James Beckford has put it, "the cult controversy is a barometer of changes taking place in a number of different societies" (1985: 11). New religious movements represent an "extreme situation" that, precisely because it is extreme, throws into sharp relief many of the assumptions hidden behind legal, cultural, and social structures. The development and operation of many NRMs in Iran has, in effect, forced societal leaders to reveal their fanaticism and partisanship, pronouncing that one set of values is favored over all others.

Those articles of the Islamic Penal Code applied against leaders and practitioners of minority faiths and NRMs are, in some cases, general and vague, which allow the Iranian criminal justice system to take advantage of this ambiguity and generality to sentence the accused using broad interpretations of the laws. This is what Herbert Hart (2012) called the "open texture of laws," meaning that there are areas of conduct where much must be developed by courts or officials, striking a balance, in light of circumstances, between competing interests that vary in weight from case to case. Because of already

---

[76] For instance, five Baha'i citizens lodged a grievance against the Municipality of Tabriz to the AJCI, requesting that the Municipality of Tabriz be obliged to allocate an exclusive place for the burial of the Baha'i deceased as a cemetery. Branch 51 of the AJCI handled the complaint and finally overruled the request in decision No. 9609970957702644, dated 31 December 2017.

[77] There has been an emergence of a dynamic jurisprudential discourse in Iran's seminaries in the past two decades with the involvement of high-ranking *faqīh*s such as Hossein-Ali Montazeri, Yousef Saane'i, Mohammad-Ebrahim Jannaati, Mohammad-Javad Alavi Boroujerdi, and some others. They have proposed new inferential practices with a focus on the inherent dignity of humankind, regardless of religion and gender, as well as on the consideration of ethics and justice as the presupposition for any jurisprudential inference (Rad Goudarzi and Najafinejad 2019; Ghobadzadeh 2022; Akbar 2023; Asghari 2023). This discourse is the first clear indication of the possible formation of a rational, human-centered, and right-oriented (*ḥaqq-madār*) *fiqh* (rather than a text-based *fiqh* emphasizing duties and responsibilities). If this nascent development can become the predominant discourse in Shi'i *fiqh*, it can help resolve the conflict between the dominant jurisprudential pattern and the rights of minorities, including religious minorities.

existing legislation and the flexibility shown by the Iranian criminal justice system in the interpretation of laws (especially vague ones), some in Iran were not convinced that more codification was needed, but others thought otherwise.[78] The debate led eventually to the passage of specific new legislation to allow even more direct and harsh control over supposedly deviant religious and spiritual movements.

Bearing in mind that today's Iran is an increasingly pluralist society, allowing a wider scope of FoRB seems worthy of consideration. If relaxing control of the religious life of the people is ever to be envisaged, solutions can be found in the Iranian Constitution and international human rights law, albeit with somewhat different interpretations than are currently accepted in Iran. On the one hand, the Constitution absolutely guarantees citizens have the right to freedom of belief in Article 23. On the other, Iran is a signatory to the ICCPR, which provides for restraints on the freedom to *manifest* one's religion or beliefs if they are *necessary* to protect public safety, order, health, or morals or the fundamental rights and freedoms of others. So, as long as the fulfillment of the manifestation of FoRB does not run afoul of the items mentioned, it should not be circumscribed and/or hampered by the government. Implementing this constitutional provision from a more open perspective could offer citizens more religious freedom and indicate that the state would not interfere with citizens' personal affairs. Whether such an approach will ever be implemented by decision-makers in Iran remains to be seen, however.

Theoretical Coda

We conclude this Element with a concise analysis of the development of the Iranian treatment of religion, and especially NRMs, with reference to prominent theories from the sociology of religion and the sociology of law. Iran represents a classic case study that supports major findings of research on religious freedom in various types of nations around the world from the viewpoint of theoretical traditions of the religious economy and the judicialization of religious freedom, as well as of theories about the role of major considerations concerning the making and functions of law. We hope that our efforts can contribute to understanding other authoritarian regimes, especially those with a strong Islamic basis, in an era of intense globalization of not only economies but also religious and spiritual ideas.

[78] Discussing these points of view on the anticult law goes beyond the confines of this Element. These comments have been documented elsewhere (see *Ruwshanā: Faṣlnāmih-yi Takhaṣṣuṣī-yi Firaq wa Adyān*, issue 77, summer 2018, pp. 8–13, and issue 82, autumn 2019, pp. 8–31, published in Iran).

The Rule of Law vs. The Rule by Law

Frequent legal assaults on religious minorities and NRMs in Iran represent the purely instrumental view of law; "law is an instrument *to serve the social good*" (Tamanaha 2007: 469, italics in original) and "[l]aw is there to serve ends designated by the lawmaker, whatever those ends might be and whatever the means required to achieve those ends" (Tamanaha 2005: 132). Such an attitude toward law in the context of intransigent disagreement over the social good leads to a battle of all against all through and over the legal order itself in a conflict to seize the implements of law and wield its coercive force against opposing groups (Tamanaha 2006a, 2007). This battle, many signs of which can be seen today, takes place in different contexts, including in legislation and in administrative, executive, and judicial actions. Law is not seen as an order of binding rules but increasingly as a tool or weapon to be manipulated to achieve desired goals. Therein lies the deep tension between legal instrumentalism and the rule of law ideal (Tamanaha 2006b).

Iran deems law as a means to maintain stability, regulate society, protect the interests of the ruling class, and strengthen and enforce the government's authority. The content of law focuses on preserving social order by the imposition of duties upon citizens. Law is not a method to limit the state's actions but a means to guarantee that the people will perform their designated duties. The ruling group may use the law to enforce its policies, but the ruling class itself is not easily restricted by law. This reflects a system known as the *rule by law*, pursuant to which "officials handle public affairs according to relevant laws, without questioning the nature of these laws" (Shih 1999: 52). The rule by law enables power holders in Iran to use law enforcement to exert social control over the populace.

Furthermore, a momentous trait of totalitarian and sometimes authoritarian regimes (such as Iran) is an exclusive, autonomous, and more or less intellectually elaborate ideology with which the leadership and the ruling elites operate. This ideology is applied as a basis and filter for every policy in all individual and societal areas. It determines the frontiers of legitimate action beyond which lies heterodoxy that can and will be negatively sanctioned. From this perspective, the politics of social control of such governments can be traced to the enactment of draconian legislation that equips the monolithic structure of centralized power with a powerful offensive weapon for surveillance, control, and suppression, intending to safeguard the ruling ideology and guarantee the regime's interests. In these governments, "law has both a repressive function, epitomised in criminal law sanctions, and an ideological function, again embodied in the criminal law's role in instantiating categories of social, political, and cultural exclusion, in modern criminological terms in labelling" (Fraser 2015: 199).

(De)judicialization of Religious Freedom

The "judicialization of religious freedom" concept (Richardson 2015, 2021) is useful in understanding the role of the judiciary in regulating religion in Iran. Richardson described the structural and historical features of societies that can operate to increase support for religious freedom. Over the past several decades in the United States and in Europe, as a result of the confluences of certain historical and structural factors, religious freedom has experienced a major increase in support, as demonstrated by congressional action in the United States and by a growing number of affirmative court decisions in Europe and America. Minority religious groups have gained support within the US Congress in reaction to a watershed 1990 US Supreme Court decision limiting claims by such groups (McGraw and Richardson 2020). However, the Supreme Court has, since that decision, changed its posture considerably on such cases by supporting many religious freedom claims in recent decisions (Richardson and McGraw 2019; Breskaya, Giordan, and Richardson 2024).

In Europe, the ECtHR has developed a very strong record over the past three decades in support of religious freedom claims brought by minority faiths, especially among newer member nations of the COE (Fokas and Richardson 2019; Evans 2001). There have been complaints that cases involving members of Islam were not handled similarly to those brought by other minority faiths in Europe (Meerschaut and Gutwirth 2008). But that concern may be dissipating somewhat, given more recent jurisprudential patterns that display an effort by the ECtHR to adopt a more religiously plural legal approach to cases involving Islam (Richardson 2019, 2021).

However, the concept of "dejudicialization of religious freedom" proposed as a corrective to theorizing about the judicialization of religious freedom by Mayrl and colleagues (Mayrl 2018; Mayrl and Venny 2021) may be more advantageous to explain what has taken place in post-Revolution Iran. Mayrl proposes that the rise of support for religious freedom that had developed after World War II in Western nations is currently dissipating under pressures from antidemocratic tendencies, resulting in the loss of autonomy and power of judicial systems. He discusses changes in interpretative rules that limit what courts can do when dealing with religious freedom claims, as well as rules that limit access to courts or offer alternative venues for dispute resolutions of cases involving religion. He also notes that courts may limit themselves when under severe pressure from other power centers in society, such as an autocratic government, a dominant church, or the military.

It is quite clear that Iran does not have an independent judiciary (UN Doc. 2022: 16), which many scholars of law and religion view as crucial to the protection of religious freedom (Richardson 2006, 2007; Finke and Martin 2014; Finke and Mataic 2021). The courts in Iran exist to implement the policies of the Shiʿite-dominated government, which identifies with and promotes a quite specific perspective of Islam. There is little recognition of constitutional guarantees that might protect older minority religions and new religions, and those provisions granting primacy to the government's view of Islam override all other considerations. Therefore, the judicialization of religious freedom does not exist in Iran, and instead there is a definite dejudicialization of religious freedom that has occurred in the past twenty years, with the courts being used as a major instrument to attack and control minority religious groups and new spiritualities. Indeed, it is safe to say that the "judicialization of politics" – the term from whence judicialization of religious freedom was derived – (Vallinder 1994; Tate and Vallinder 1995; Hirschl 2006, 2011) also does not exist in Iran. The state apparatus, in conjunction with the Shiʿite clergy, attempts to dominate all aspects of Iranian society. This is similar to what has happened in a number of countries, such as China, post-Communist Russia, Saudi Arabia, and now Afghanistan, where the government favors a dominant faith or ideology.

Iranian courts are used to enforce the official governmental view of all aspects of life, particularly religion. Thus the prerequisites for the development and maintenance of religious freedom and other civil and political rights do not now exist in Iran. Beyond doubt, courts in Iran, inter alia, suppress potential threats to the political establishment and the *mainline interpretation* of the official religion. Despite constitutional guarantees of judicial independence, the Iranian judiciary is designed as a judicial-political institution that is responsible not only for the administration of justice (as defined by the authorities in Iran) but also for the implementation of the ideological line advocated by the conservative establishment. Courts in Iran are often not impartial actors and their power emanates from their partiality in favor of the government's Islamic ideocracy. We argue that the regime's use of courts reveals the importance of legal frameworks to authoritarian and totalitarian regimes as a device for apparently justifying repression by constructing a narrative of threats to the state and presenting the masses with an exercise of state power through apparently legitimate means anchored in the politico-legal order. Furthermore, when willing to comply with authority and/or turn a blind eye to the effects of their judgments by applying repressive legislation without objection, judges cease acting as a *balancer* between the government and citizens and become active in the former's exertion of power to violate the private space of individual life.

Religious Economy (Supply-Side Theory)

The "economics of religion" or the "religious economy" theory developed over many years with much research by scholars such as Roger Finke, Rodney Stark, and Laurence Iannaccone, among others. The groundwork for the religious economy thesis draws on the ideas of three prominent scholars of the eighteenth century: Voltaire (1694–1778), Adam Smith (1723–1790), and David Hume (1711–1776). Voltaire, in 1733, held up English toleration of dissident Protestant sects as a model for the French (even though the English did not extend the same tolerance to Catholics). He praised the rationalism, productivity, and, particularly, the religious diversity of England, which he saw as enabling a pragmatic disinterest in the ceremonies and beliefs of others: "If one religion only were allowed in *England*, the Government would very possibly become arbitrary; if there were but two, the people would cut one another's throats; but as there are such a multitude, they all live happy and in peace" (Voltaire 1894: 44, italics in original). This mutually beneficial cosmopolitanism was, in his eyes, best exemplified by the London Stock Exchange, where Christians, Jews, and Muslims transacted business with each other as though they all professed the same religion.

A few decades later in 1776, Adam Smith echoed Voltaire's concerns about religious monopolies and his assurances about plurality: "The interested and active zeal of religious teachers can be dangerous and troublesome only where there is, either but one sect tolerated in the society, or where the whole of a large society is divided into two or three great sects" (1937: 745). He went on to explain, however, that the "zeal must be altogether innocent where the society is divided into two or three hundred, or perhaps into as many [as a] thousand small sects, of which no one could be considerable enough to disturb the public tranquillity" (745). For Smith, the argument was based on theoretical common sense rather than personal experiences: if sects are numerous enough, no single sect is large enough to be harmful. The obvious question that follows, of course, is how are the numerous sects generated? For Smith, the answer is simple: "[I]f the government was perfectly decided both to let them all alone and to oblige them all to let alone one another, there is little danger that they would not of their own accord subdivide themselves fast enough, so as soon to become sufficiently numerous" (746). "Letting them all alone" allowed for an open propagating of faith by multiple religious groups; obliging the religions to "let alone one another" ensured that no single religion would hold power over another religious movement. Religious plurality, for Smith, was the natural state of affairs, and such plurality resulted in public tranquility.

David Hume offered a similar observation, published posthumously in 1779, concurring that the government must leave the various religious groups alone and must require all of them to leave one another alone as well:

> If [a magistrate] admits only one religion among his subjects, he must sacrifice, to an uncertain prospect of tranquillity, every consideration of public liberty, science, reason, industry, and even his own independency. If he gives indulgence to several sects, which is the wiser maxim, he must preserve a very philosophical indifference to all of them, and carefully restrain the pretensions of the prevailing sect; otherwise he can expect nothing but endless disputes, quarrels, factions, persecutions, and civil commotions. (2007: 181)

Hume brings an important nuance to the discussion by drawing attention to the fact that constraints must be placed on the "pretensions of the prevailing sect." Without such constraints, Hume contends, the predominant religion will seek to control other religions. Thus Hume and Smith are suggesting that religions must be protected from both the state and one another.

Iran demonstrates a major finding of the religious economy tradition: Muslim nations are often much more restrictive than other nations toward minority faiths (Grim and Finke 2011; Finke and Martin 2014; Fox 2016). The confluence of political and religious power structures in Iran that has evolved over the decades since the Revolution clearly illustrates findings from the religious economy literature concerning what happens when a dominant religion is overtaken by or forms an alliance with the political structure of the society (Stark and Finke 2000; Finke 2013; Finke and Martin 2014; Mataic and Finke 2019). In part this occurs because the authoritarian leadership of Iran, in collaboration with the national intelligence–security apparatus, oversees judges and local officials, among others, to ensure that the preferred view of Islam is implemented to the detriment of NRMs and older minority faiths that have existed for longer periods of time in Iran.

Although the minority religious and spiritual groups that are threatened and discriminated against so forcefully are quite small, Iranian authorities view them as a threat to the national government and the Islamic culture of Iran because of their origins, cultural proximity to the mainstream, and attractiveness to certain segments of the population. Also, these newer groups can be used as "convenient scapegoats" to help build political support. When one religion is closely associated with the state, this makes the state more likely to discriminate against other religions. For the state, this alliance with the dominant religion can provide increased popular support and legitimation from religious people and institutions, as well as increased loyalty from both. For the dominant religion, the alliance gives it a competitive advantage over other religious and cultural groups by providing more resources from the state and formal support for its institutions, as well as imposing restrictions on religious competitors. As a result, the religious economy model suggests that "government favoritism" – subsidies, privileges, support, or favorable sanctions furnished by the state for one or a select group of religions – will result in fewer resources for others and is a strong predictor of restrictions on religious freedom. This explanation also helps us understand compliance gaps between states' promises and practices. When the state and the dominant religion ally, the state will be under increased pressure to restrict the activities of the alternative religions deemed as unwanted religious competitors. Consequently, the Iranian religiopolitical establishment has decided that those alternatives to official Islam must be suppressed, and the entire institutional structure of the state (especially the mass media and the judiciary) seems devoted to this aim. Part of the motivation of the government to exert total control over minority religious groups and noninstitutionalized spiritualities may derive from growing disquiet among some segments of the populace and the developing interest in alternative forms of religion and spirituality discussed earlier in this Element. But it seems clear that the major thrust is simply to exert control over every aspect of life in Iran by a thoroughly authoritarian government. Thus our detailed case study of Iran offers additional support for the major findings of other researchers studying similar regimes in the region and elsewhere.

Structural Contradictions and "Making Law"

From the sociology of law perspective, William Chambliss's theory of "structural contradictions" is quite applicable to the situation of Iran concerning religion and religiosity-related statutory developments. Chambliss's groundbreaking theorizing (1979a, 1979b, 1993; Chambliss and Seidman 1982) is concentrated on the *dialectic processes* whereby law and social policy develop. For him, the vocabulary, theory, and methodology suitable for the study of law and society should begin not with vast impersonal forces sweeping across empty heads and determining human action, but with thinking, choosing, and creating human beings. Society is a collection of human beings, not an entity with its own needs, force, and consciousness. It consists of people acting together in repetitive patterns shaped but not determined by the constraints of a particular historical period. Chambliss's theory emphasizes human agency and decries mechanistic and reifying theories that denigrate human volition and do not take human decision-making into account. He proposes a theory that focuses on how people in positions to influence and create law try to resolve the *dilemmas*[79] and *conflicts* arising from the existence of *contradictions* (Chambliss 1988: 130).[80] Chambliss sees lawmaking as "a *process* aimed at the resolution of contradictions, conflicts, and dilemmas that are historically grounded in time and space and inherent in the structure of a particular political, economic, and social structure" (Chambliss 1993: 9).

To summarize Chambliss's theoretical approach, contradictions result in visible and concrete conflicts between interest groups. Dealing with those conflicts produces dilemmas for the state to resolve. The state apparatus must decide which interests to defend or what kind of compromise to work out between competing interests. Not all conflicts can be addressed at the same time, and the very process of containing one conflict often causes others to emerge. Societal leadership's attention must focus on the most acute conflicts, those causing or likely soon to cause tears in the social fabric. If such conflicts are ignored, the legitimacy of the leadership and potentially of the larger political structure could be questioned. On the other hand, since no resolution can be perfect given the multiple forces confronting any given society, the dilemma often comes down to choosing the lesser evil (i.e., the least problematic resolution) and finding a means to reach that tentative resolution. How conflicts and dilemmas are constructed, portrayed, and resolved depends in large part on the hegemonic and alternative ideological orientations available and the relative salience of the various contradictions in evidence at that point in time.

Often the immediate response for resolving conflicts and dilemmas is to make changes in the legal domain, including especially creation of new laws. Laws, however, tend to respond to specific conflicts rather than addressing the contradictions that underline them. This is because "[t]he contradictions are too

79 This concept refers to "the uncertainties faced by various actors, and especially the political leadership, concerning the best way to resolve conflicts" (Zatz 1994: 40).

80 The starting point for understanding criminal law is the articulation of existing contradictions in a particular historical epoch. "A contradiction is established in a particular historical period when the working out of the logic of the extant political, economic, ideological, and social relations must necessarily destroy some fundamental aspects of existing social relations" (Chambliss 1993: 9). "A contradiction exists in a given set of social relationships (political, social, economic, and ideological) when, in the normal course of events, existing social relations simultaneously maintain the status quo and produce the contradictions necessary to transform it – that is, when conforming to one set of demands, goals, or institutionalized processes creates situations that are fundamentally antagonistic to the existing social relations" (Chambliss 2008: 289). Under these circumstances, contradictions tend to intensify with time and cannot be resolved within the existing social framework. Every historical era, every society, and every human group in the process of constructing ways to survive invariably creates contradictory forces and tendencies that serve as an unseen force moving the group toward new social, political, and economic relations. Change is thus an inexorable part of every human group.

fundamental: to resolve the contradictions necessarily requires changing fundamentally the organizational form of political, economic, and social relations" (Chambliss 1988: 304). Hence, solving basic contradictions is difficult and demands more than a legislature can do by itself. That being so, laws are only temporary resolutions because in the resolution of particular conflicts and dilemmas, assuming that the basic contradictions are not resolved, inevitably the seeds for further conflicts arise. Often, resolutions of particular conflicts and dilemmas not only create further conflicts but spotlight as well other contradictions that were heretofore less salient (see Figure 1). As a result, other new and reformulated contradictions are revealed, other conflicts arise, and a multitude of dilemmas and struggles are ensured, which must then be resolved. Long-term resolutions can come about only if and when the fundamental contradictions generating the conflicts are eradicated. Therefore, a continuous dialectic process of development of law and policy occurs in any society, and laws serve as temporary resolutions to conflicts and dilemmas that are rooted in structural contradictions.

The concept of "triggering events," introduced by sociologists Galliher and colleagues (Galliher and Basilick 1979; Galliher and Cross 1983), is an important addition to the basic structural contradictions theory that has been accepted by Chambliss. This notion refers to events that "actually lead to passage of a specific piece of legislation" (McGarrell and Castellano 1993: 349).

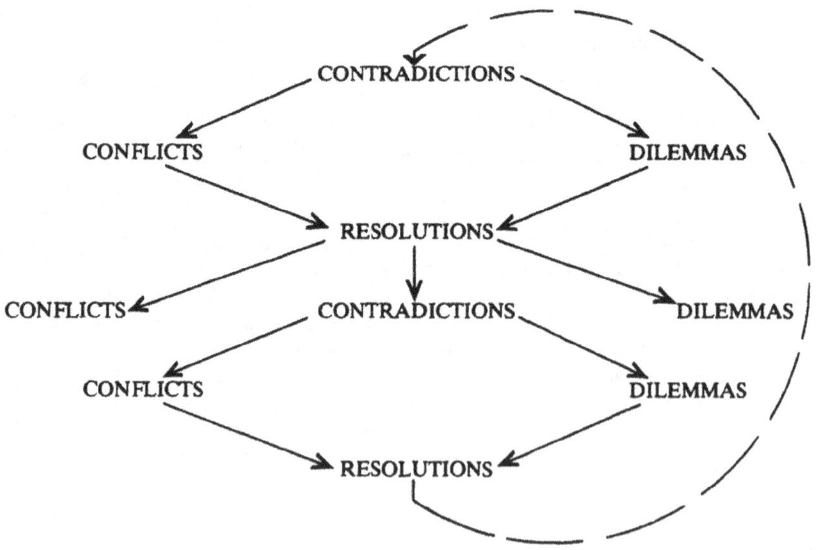

Figure 1 Schematic diagram depicting the processes in Chambliss's model. Image used with permission.

Chambliss's theory has been expanded and applied in many different settings since it was propounded. For example, it has recently been used to aid understanding of the development of anti-Shariʿa legislative efforts in the United States, Canada, and Australia (Richardson 2023) as well as the development of anticult legislation in France (Adeliyan Tous, Richardson, and Taghipour 2023). The situation in Iran offers an opportunity to apply these ideas to a Muslim-majority nation that has undertaken major efforts to control potential competitors and promote its particular interpretation of Islam.

Final Observations

The societal situation in Iran today may be analogous to that Chambliss (1964) discovered in his study of the development of vagrancy laws in historical England since there was no role for judicial decisions – there were few, if any, functioning autonomous courts with any authority to overrule laws that were proclaimed by vested interest groups and societal authorities such as monarchies. The Supreme Leader was and is the ultimate authority in Iran, and courts and all other institutions in Iranian society are called on to implement his edicts. Nonetheless, there were contradictions within the legal structure of Iranian society vis-à-vis religion. There were clear edicts in the Constitution and in laws and normative practices establishing the primacy of a specific version of Islam. But, as demonstrated in this Element, many members of the citizenry are not interested in following the "party line" concerning the specific version of Islam promoted by the state's cleric-dominated apparatus. Indeed, many citizens are either merely losing interest in abiding by official edicts regarding Islam or turning to irreligion or developing an interest in religious and spiritual alternatives based/not based on Islam, some of which were and are quite radical when compared to the Shiʿite version of Islam being promulgated. This developing skepticism of the official line on Islam could be considered a major impetus to the lengthy social control and legislative efforts detailed in Section 4 and thus can be viewed as a triggering set of events in the parlance of Chambliss's theoretical scheme.

The contradictions and conflicts discussed throughout this Element were of obvious concern to Iranian authorities, evidenced by several major efforts to develop more rigorous legislation to resolve the dilemma and avoid further conflict within society. The lengthy machinations detailed herein certainly demonstrate the dialectical nature of the process of trying to resolve the contradictions within Iranian society regarding the religious feelings and beliefs of the citizenry. Only time will reveal if the resolution finally obtained in 2021 is a lasting one that settles the perceived contradictions in Iranian society or, perhaps more accurately, if what happened is just another temporary solution that will lead to continuing conflicts.

References

Adeliyan Tous, S., Richardson, J. T., and Taghipour, A. (2023). "Using Law to Limit Religious Freedom: The Case of New Religious Movements in France." *Religions*, 14(7), Article No. 887, 1–29.

Afshari, R. (2011). *Human Rights in Iran: The Abuse of Cultural Relativism*. Philadelphia: University of Pennsylvania Press.

Ahdar, R., and Leigh, I. (2013). *Religious Freedom in the Liberal State*, 2nd ed. Oxford: Oxford University Press.

Ahmadi, E., and Shah-Hoseini, S. (2017). *Dar Qalamruw-i Sāyih-hā: Justār-hā-yī dar Rawān-shināsī-yi Firqih-hā*, 2nd printing, 2nd ed. Tehran: Nashr-i Nārgul.

Akbar, A. (2023). "Change from within: Shia Seminarians' Responses to Contemporary Religious and Social Challenges." *Journal of Religious History*, 47(2), 222–42.

Ala Hamoudi, H. (2019). "Beyond the State and the Hawza: Legal Pluralism and the Ironies of Shiʾi Law." In J. L. Neo, A. A. Jamal, and D. P. S. Goh, eds., *Regulating Religion in Asia: Norms, Modes, and Challenges*. Cambridge: Cambridge University Press, pp. 298–312.

Amanat, A. (2005). *Resurrection and Renewal: The Making of the Babi Movement in Iran, 1844–1850*. Los Angeles, CA: Kalimát Press.

Amini, T. (2012). *Asnād-i Bahāʾīyān-i Iran: az Sāl-i 1320 ta Pāyān-i Sāl-i 1331*. Stockholm: Nashr-i Bārān.

Amini, T. (2014). *Asnād-i Bahāʾīyān-i Iran: az Sāl-i 1332 ta Inqilāb-i Islāmī*. Stockholm: Nashr-i Bārān.

Amirpur, K. (2012). "Iran's Policy towards Jewish Iranians and the State of Israel: Is the Present Iranian State Islamofascist?" *Die Welt des Islams*, 52(3–4), 370–99.

An-Naʿim, A. A. (2009). "A Theory of Islam, State, and Society." In K. Vogt, L. Larsen, and C. Moe, eds., *New Directions in Islamic Thought: Exploring Reform and Muslim Tradition*. London: I. B. Tauris, pp. 145–62.

Anthony, D. (1999). "Pseudoscience and Minority Religions: An Evaluation of the Brainwashing Theories of Jean-Marie Abgrall." *Social Justice Research*, 12(4), 421–56.

Anvāri, M. (2012). Barrasī-yi Zamīnih-hā wa Awāmil-i Gustarish-i Āthār-i Paulo Coelho dar Iran. Master's Thesis, Baqir al-Olum University, Qom.

Arzt, D. E. (1995). "Heroes or Heretics: Religious Dissidents under Islamic Law." *Wisconsin International Law Journal*, 14(2), 349–421.

Arzt, D. E. (2002). "The Role of Compulsion in Islamic Conversion: *Jihad*, *Dhimma* and *Ridda*." *Buffalo Human Rights Law Review*, 8, 15–44.

Asghari, S. A. (2023). "Understanding Human Dignity in Shi'i Islam: Debates, Challenges, and Solutions for Contemporary Issues." *Religions*, 14(4), Article No. 505, 1–12.

Asim, M. (2023). "Iranian Constitution Under Pro-Center Dogmatic Authoritarianism and Pro-Persian Cosmopolitanism, and Its Impacts on Ethno-sectarian and Ethno-linguistic Minorities." In S. B. Hosseini, ed., *Ethnic Religious Minorities in Iran*. Singapore: Palgrave Macmillan, pp. 13–44.

Bahá'í International Community. (1993). *The Bahá'í Question: Iran's Secret Blueprint for the Destruction of a Religious Community*. New York: Bahá'í International Community Publications.

Bahá'í International Community. (2023). *The Bahá'í Question: Persecution and Resilience in Iran*. New York: Bahá'í International Community, United Nations Office.

Bahar, S. (1992). "Khomeinism, the Islamic Republic of Iran, and International Law: The Relevance of Islamic Political Ideology." *Harvard International Law Journal*, 33(1), 145–90.

Banakar, R., and Ziaee, K. (2018). "The Life of the Law in the Islamic Republic of Iran." *Iranian Studies*, 51(5), 717–46.

Barker, E. (1984). *Making of a Moonie: Choice or Brainwashing?* Oxford: Basil Blackwell.

Barker, E. (1989). *New Religious Movements: A Practical Introduction*. London: Her Majesty's Stationery Office.

Becker, H. S. (2018). *Outsiders: Studies in the Sociology of Deviance*. New York: Free Press.

Beckford, J. A. (1985). *Cult Controversies: The Societal Response to New Religious Movements*. London: Tavistock.

Behdasht Maʿnavi News Website. (2019). "Waḍʿīyat-i Nashr-i Kitāb-hā-yi Intiqādī-yi ʿIrfān-hā-yi Kādhib." 2 August. https://behdashtemanavi.com/?p=4248. (accessed on 5 August 2023).

Black, D. (1993). *The Social Structure of Right and Wrong*. San Diego, CA: Academic Press.

Breskaya, O., Giordan, G., and Richardson, J. T. (2024). *A Sociology of Religious Freedom*. Oxford: Oxford University Press.

Carmichael, J. (2012). "Social Control." *Oxford Bibliographies Online (OBO) in Sociology*. https://doi.org/10.1093/OBO/9780199756384-0048.

Chambliss, W. J. (1964). "A Sociological Analysis of the Law of Vagrancy." *Social Problems*, 12(1), 46–67.

Chambliss, W. J. (1979a). "On Lawmaking." *British Journal of Law and Society*, 6(2), 149–71.

Chambliss, W. J. (1979b). "Contradictions and Conflicts in Law Creation." In S. Spitzer, ed., *Research in Law and Sociology*. Vol. 2. Greenwich, CT: JAI Press, pp. 3–27.

Chambliss, W. J. (1988). *Exploring Criminology*. New York: Macmillan.

Chambliss, W. J. (1993). "On Lawmaking." In W. J. Chambliss and M. S. Zatz, eds., *Making Law: The State, the Law, and Structural Contradictions*. Bloomington: Indiana University Press, pp. 3–35.

Chambliss, W. J. (2008). "Crime and Structural Contradictions." In R. D. Crutchfield, C. E. Kubrin, G. S. Bridges, and J. S. Weis, eds., *Crime: Readings*, 3rd ed. Thousand Oaks, CA: Sage, pp. 289–95.

Chambliss, W. J., and Seidman, R. B. (1982). *Law, Order, and Power*. Reading, MA: Addison-Wesley.

Choksy, J. K. (2012). "Non-Muslim Religious Minorities in Contemporary Iran." *Iran and the Caucasus*, 16(3), 271–99.

Dillon, J., and Richardson, J. T. (1994). "The 'Cult' Concept: A Politics of Representation Analysis." *SYZYGY: Journal of Alternative Religion and Culture*, 3(3–4), 185–97.

Doostdar, A. (2018). *The Iranian Metaphysicals: Explorations in Science, Islam, and the Uncanny*. Princeton, NJ: Princeton University Press.

Evans, C. (2001). *Freedom of Religion under the European Convention on Human Rights*. Oxford: Oxford University Press.

Faʿʿālī, M. (2010). *Naqd wa Barrasī-yi Junbish-hā-yi Nuw-ẓuhūr-i Maʿnawī*, 8 vols. Tehran: National Youth Organization.

Faʿʿālī, M. (2022). *Āftāb wa Sāyih-hā: Nigarishī bar Jaryān-hā-yi Nuw-ẓuhūr-i Maʿnawīyat-girā*, 32nd printing, 5th ed. Qom: Nashr-i Tīmās.

Farshchi, E. (2024). "New Religious Movements in Iran: Determinants of Toleration and Repression by the State." *Nova Religio*, 27(4), 31–52.

Fazel Lankarani, M., and Ghasemi, M. (2022). "Tafsīrī Nuw az Naẓarīyih-yi 'al-Islām huwa al-hukūma' wa Mustanadāt-i Ān." *Muṭāliʿāt-i Fiqh-i Sīyāsat*, 2(1), 7–25.

Finke, R. (2013). "Origins and Consequences of Religious Restrictions: A Global Overview." *Sociology of Religion*, 74(3), 297–313.

Finke, R., and Martin, R. R. (2014). "Ensuring Liberties: Understanding State Restrictions on Religious Freedoms." *Journal for the Scientific Study of Religion*, 53(4), 687–705.

Finke, R., and Mataic, D. R. (2019). "Promises, Practices, and Consequences of Religious Freedom: A Global Overview." *University of St. Thomas Law Journal*, 15(3), 587–606.

Finke, R., and Mataic, D. R. (2021). "Reconciling State Promises and Practices: Constitutional Promises and Discrimination against Religious Minorities." *Social Compass*, 68(3), 301–20.

Fischer, M. M. J. (2003). *Iran: From Religious Dispute to Revolution*. Madison: University of Wisconsin Press.

Fokas, E., and Richardson, J. T. (2019). *The European Court of Human Rights and Minority Religions: Messages Generated and Messages Received*. London: Routledge.

Foltz, R. (2011). "Zoroastrians in Iran: What Future in the Homeland?" *Middle East Journal*, 65(1), 73–84.

Fox, J. (2015). *Political Secularism, Religion, and the State: A Time Series Analysis of Worldwide Data*. Cambridge: Cambridge University Press.

Fox, J. (2016). *The Unfree Exercise of Religion: A World Survey of Discrimination against Religious Minorities*. Cambridge: Cambridge University Press.

Fox, J. (2017). "Political Secularism and Democracy in Theory and Practice." In P. Zuckerman and J. R. Shook, eds., *The Oxford Handbook of Secularism*. New York: Oxford University Press, pp. 103–22.

Fox, J. (2018). *An Introduction to Religion and Politics: Theory and Practice*, 2nd ed. London: Routledge.

Fox, J. (2020). *Thou Shalt Have No Other Gods before Me: Why Governments Discriminate against Religious Minorities*. Cambridge: Cambridge University Press.

Fox, J. (2023). "Do Religion Clauses in Constitutions Predict Government-Based Discrimination against Religious Minorities?" *Religions*, 14(1), Article No. 92, 1–33.

Fox, J., and Flores, D. (2009). "Religions, Constitutions, and the State: A Cross-National Study." *The Journal of Politics*, 71(4), 1499–1513.

Fox, J., James, P., and Li, Y. (2009). "State Religion and Discrimination Against Ethnic Minorities." *Nationalism and Ethnic Politics*, 15(2), 189–210.

Fox, J., and Topor, L. (2021). *Why Do People Discriminate against Jews?* Oxford: Oxford University Press.

Fraser, D. (2015). "Through the Looking Glass: Thinking About and Working Through Fascist Criminal Law." In S. Skinner, ed., *Fascism and Criminal Law: History, Theory, Continuity*. Oxford: Hart, pp. 197–208.

Galliher, J. F., and Basilick, L. (1979). "Utah's Liberal Drug Laws: Structural Foundations and Triggering Events." *Social Problems*, 26(3), 284–97.

Galliher, J. F., and Cross, J. R. (1983). *Morals Legislation Without Morality: The Case of Nevada*. New Brunswick, NJ: Rutgers University Press.

Ghanea, N., and Pinto, T. A., eds. (2020). "Special Issue: Limitations to Freedom of Religion or Belief in Theory and Practice." *Religion & Human Rights*, 15(1–2), 1–206.

Ghobadzadeh, N. (2022). "Wasatiyya Discourse in Shi'i Islam: Ayatollah Montazeri and Human Rights Jurisprudence." *Religions*, 13(2), Article No. 126, 1–17.

Gholamizadeh Behbahani, S. (2006). "Dīndārī-yi Muwāzī": Muṭāliʿih-yi Dalāyil-i Jāmiʿih-shināsānih-yi Piydāyish-i Ān. Master's Thesis, Al-Zahra University, Tehran.

Gholamizadeh Behbahani, S. (2016). Les Raisons Sociologiques de l'Émergence des Nouveaux Mouvements Religieux en Iran: de la Religion Capturée à la Religion Abritée. PhD Dissertation, Université de Strasbourg.

Godazgar, H. (2020). "From 'Islamism' to 'Spiritualism'? The Contemporary Individualization of 'Religion' in Contemporary Iran." *Religions*, 11(1), Article No. 32, 1–26.

Golestaneh, S. (2023). "And the Master Answered? Deferrals of Authority in Contemporary Sufism in Iran." *Iranian Studies*, 56(2), 365–86.

Gouda, M., and Gutmann, J. (2021). "Islamic Constitutions and Religious Minorities." *Public Choice*, 186(3–4), 243–65.

Grim, B. J., and Finke, R. (2006). "International Religion Indexes: Government Regulation, Government Favoritism, and Social Regulation of Religion." *Interdisciplinary Journal of Research on Religion*, 2, Article No. 1, 1–40.

Grim, B. J., and Finke, R. (2011). *The Price of Freedom Denied: Religious Persecution and Conflict in the Twenty-First Century*. Cambridge: Cambridge University Press.

Gunn, T. J. (2011). "Permissible Limitations on the Freedom of Religion or Belief." In J. Witte and M. Ch. Green, eds., *Religion and Human Rights: An Introduction*. New York: Oxford University Press, pp. 254–68.

Gunn, T. J. (2020). "Do Human Rights Have a Secular, Individualistic & Anti-Islamic Bias?" *Daedalus*, 149(3), 148–69.

Gunn, T. J., and Sabil, O. (2023). "Sharī'a in the Qur'an: A Word Meaning 'Law' or a Metaphor Evoking 'Path'?" In A. Possamai, J. T. Richardson, and B. S. Turner, eds., *The Sociology of Shari'a: Case Studies from around the World*, 2nd ed. Cham: Springer, pp. 23–54.

Gunner, G. (2023). "Religious Freedom as a Human Right." In M. J. H. Bhuiyan and C. M. Zoethout, eds., *Freedom of Religion and Religious Pluralism*. Leiden: Brill, pp. 79–100.

Hakim, M. A. (1998). "The Use of Islam as a Political Legitimization Tool: The Bangladesh Experience, 1972–1990." *Asian Journal of Political Science*, 6(2), 98–117.

Hamidieh, B. (2020). *Darsnāmih-yi Naqd-i Maʿnawīyat-hā-yi Nuw-padīd*. Qom: Muʾassisih-yi Būstān-i Kitāb.

Hart, H. L. A. (2012). *The Concept of Law*, 3rd ed. Oxford: Oxford University Press.

Hasannia, A., Fazeli, Z., and Fazeli, M. R. (2023). "Iranian Jews' Tendency to Religious Visibility and Adapted Coexistence." In S. B. Hosseini, ed., *Ethnic Religious Minorities in Iran*. Singapore: Palgrave Macmillan, pp. 109–45.

Hasanzadeh Tabatabaei, S. M. (2019). "Barrasī-yi Nufūdh-i Tafakkur-i Nuwīn bi ʿUnwān-i Faʿʿāl-tarīn Jaryān-i Maʿnawī dar Iran (bar Mabnā-yi Taḥlīl-i Āthār-i Niwīsandigān-i Muhim)." *Muṭāliʿāt-i Maʿnawī*, 8(1), 87–118.

Hashemi, N. (2014). "Rethinking Religion and Political Legitimacy across the Islam–West Divide." *Philosophy and Social Criticism*, 40 (4–5), 439–47.

Heelas, P. (1996). *The New Age Movement: The Celebration of the Self and the Sacralization of Modernity*. Oxford: Blackwell.

Hirschl, R. (2006). "The New Constitutionalism and the Judicialization of Pure Politics Worldwide." *Fordham Law Review*, 75(2), 721–53.

Hirschl, R. (2010). *Constitutional Theocracy*. Cambridge, MA: Harvard University Press.

Hirschl, R. (2011). "The Judicialization of Politics." In R. E. Goodin, ed., *The Oxford Handbook of Political Science*. Oxford: Oxford University Press, pp. 253–74.

Hirschl, R. (2012). "The Political Economy of Constitutionalism in a Non-Secularist World." In T. Ginsburg, ed., *Comparative Constitutional Design*. Cambridge: Cambridge University Press, pp. 164–92.

Hmimnat, S. (2021). "Morocco's State Islam: Securitization, Legitimization, and Authoritarian (-Neoliberal) Modernization." *Journal of South Asian and Middle Eastern Studies*, 44(4), 1–24.

Human Rights Council. (2014). *National Report Submitted in Accordance with Paragraph 5 of the Annex to Human Rights Council Resolution 16/21, Iran (Islamic Republic of)*. A/HRC/WG.6/20/IRN/1. 4 August.

Hume, David. (2007). *Dialogues Concerning Natural Religion and Other Writings*. Cambridge: Cambridge University Press.

Introvigne, M. (2022). *Brainwashing: Reality or Myth?* Cambridge: Cambridge University Press.

IRNA. (2014). "Muʿāwin-i Awwal-i Quwwih-yi Qaḍāʾīyih: Ittihām-i Bahāʾīyān-i Dastgīrshodih Jāsūsī Ast." 10 April. www.irna.ir/news/81116385 (accessed on 26 September 2022).

Jaberian, N., Rabiei, A., Mohaddesi Gilvaei, H., and Zahedi Mazandarani, M. (2017). "A Sociological Look at the Growth of the Emerging Spirituality in Tabriz." *Journal of Iranian Cultural Research*, 10(2), 119–50.

Jahanbegloo, R. (2011). "Iran and the Democratic Struggle in the Middle East." *Middle East Law and Governance*, 3(1–2), 126–35.

Jaspal, R. (2013). "Anti-Semitism and anti-Zionism in Iran." *Israel Affairs*, 19(2), 231–58.

Jaspal, R. (2015). "Antisemitism and Anti-Zionism in Iran: The Effects of Identity, Threat, and Political Trust." *Contemporary Jewry*, 35(3), 211–35.

Kadivar, M. (2021). *Blasphemy and Apostasy in Islam: Debates in Shiʿa Jurisprudence*. Translated by H. Mavani. Edinburgh: Edinburgh University Press.

Karawan, I. A. (1992). "Monarchs, Mullas, and Marshals: Islamic Regimes?" *ANNALS of the American Academy of Political and Social Science*, 524(1), 103–19.

Karlberg, M. (2010). "Constructive Resilience: The Bahá'í Response to Oppression." *Peace & Change*, 35(2), 222–57.

Kazemipur, A., and Rezaei, A. (2003). "Religious Life under Theocracy: The Case of Iran." *Journal for the Scientific Study of Religion*, 42(3), 347–61.

Khamenei, S. A. (2023). *Ajwibat al-Istiftāʾāt*. Tehran: Intishārāt-i Inqilāb-i Islāmī.

Khomeini, S. R. (2009). *Kitāb al-Bayʿ*. Vol. 2, 3rd printing. Qom: Muʾassasat Tanẓīm wa-Nashr Āthār al-Imām al-Khumaynī.

Khomeini, S. R. (2013). *Taḥrīr al-Wasīla*. 2 vols., 3rd printing. Qom: Muʾassasat Tanẓīm wa-Nashr Āthār al-Imām al-Khumaynī.

Khoshnood, A. (2019). "Shah of Iran and the Baha'is: The Importance of Transparency." *Contemporary Review of the Middle East*, 6(2), 212–15.

Künkler, M. (2013). "The Special Court of the Clergy (*Dādgāh-e Vizheh-ye Ruhāniyat*) and the Repression of Dissident Clergy in Iran." In S. A. Arjomand and N. J. Brown, eds., *The Rule of Law, Islam, and Constitutional Politics in Egypt and Iran*. Albany: State University of New York Press, pp. 57–100.

Kuru, A. T. (2019). *Islam, Authoritarianism, and Underdevelopment: A Global and Historical Comparison*. Cambridge: Cambridge University Press.

Lewis, B. (2014). *The Jews of Islam*. Princeton, NJ: Princeton University Press.

Litvak, M. (2017). "Iranian Antisemitism and the Holocaust." In A. McElligott and J. Herf, eds., *Antisemitism Before and Since the Holocaust: Altered Contexts and Recent Perspectives*. Cham: Palgrave Macmillan, pp. 205–29.

Litvak, M. (2020). "Modern Antisemitism in Iran: Old Themes and New Trends." In A. Lange, K. Mayerhofer, D. Porat, and L. H. Schiffman, eds., *An End to Antisemitism: Confronting Antisemitism from the Perspectives of Christianity, Islam, and Judaism*. Berlin: De Gruyter, pp. 301–20.

Litvak, M. (2021). *Know Thy Enemy: Evolving Attitudes towards "Others" in Modern Shiʿi Thought and Practice*. Leiden: Brill.

Lombardi, C. B. (2013). "Designing Islamic Constitutions: Past Trends and Options for a Democratic Future." *International Journal of Constitutional Law*, 11(3), 615–45.

MacEoin, D. (2009). *The Messiah of Shiraz: Studies in Early and Middle Babism*. Leiden: Brill.

Madeley, J. T. S. (2003). "A Framework for the Comparative Analysis of Church–State Relations in Europe." *West European Politics*, 26(1), 23–50.

Manchi Chao, M., Zhang, Z., and Chiu, C. (2008). "Personal and Collective Culpability Judgment: A Functional Analysis of East Asian–North American Differences." *Journal of Cross-Cultural Psychology*, 39(6), 730–44.

Martin, D. (1984). "The Persecution of the Bahá'ís of Iran, 1844–1984." *Baha'i Studies*, 12–13, 1–88.

Mataic, D. R. (2018). "Countries Mimicking Neighbors: The Spatial Diffusion of Governmental Restrictions on Religion." *Journal for the Scientific Study of Religion*, 57(2), 221–37.

Mataic, D. R., and Finke, R. (2019). "Compliance Gaps and the Failed Promise of Religious Freedoms." *Religion, State & Society*, 47(1), 124–50.

Mayer, A. E. (1996). "Islamic Rights or Human Rights: An Iranian Dilemma." *Iranian Studies*, 29(3–4), 269–96.

Mayer, A. E. (2018). *Islam and Human Rights: Tradition and Politics*, 5th ed. New York: Routledge.

Mayrl, D. (2018). "The Judicialization of Religious Freedom: An Institutionalist Approach." *Journal for the Scientific Study of Religion*, 57(3), 514–30.

Mayrl, D., and Venny, D. (2021). "The Dejudicialization of Religious Freedom?" *Social Compass*, 68(3), 342–58.

Mazaheri Seif, H. (2016). *Āsīb-shināsī-yi Shibh-i Junbish-hā-yi Maʿnawī*. Qom: Ṣahbā-yi Yaqīn.

Mazaheri Seif, H. (2020). *Jaryān-shināsī-yi Intiqādī-yi ʿIrfān-hā-yi Nuw-ẓuhūr*, 6th printing. Qom: Islamic Sciences and Culture Academy.

McGarrell, E. F., and Castellano, T. C. (1993). "An Integrative Conflict Model of the Criminal Law Formation Process." *Journal of Research in Crime and Delinquency*, 28(2), 174–96.

McGraw, B., and Richardson, J. T. (2020). "Religious Regulation in the United States." In P. A. Djupe, M. J. Rozell, and T. G. Jelen, eds., *The Oxford Encyclopedia of Politics and Religion*. New York: Oxford University Press, pp. 1443–67.

Meerschaut, K., and Gutwirth, S. (2008). "Legal Pluralism and Islam in the Scales of the European Court of Human Rights: The Limits of Categorical Balancing." In E. Brems, ed., *Conflicts between Fundamental Rights*. Antwerp: Intersentia, pp. 431–65.

Menashri, D. (2006). "Iran, Israel and the Middle East Conflict." *Israel Affairs*, 12(1), 107–22.

Meral, Z. (2013). "Religious Minorities and Conversion as National Security Threats in Turkey and Iran." In D. M. Kirkham, ed., *State Responses to Minority Religions*. Burlington, VT: Ashgate, pp. 31–44.

Milani, S. (2016). "The Situation of the Bahá'í Minority in Iran and the Existing Legal Framework." *Journal of International Affairs*, 69(2), 137–48.

Miller, D. A., and Johnstone, P. (2015). "Believers in Christ from a Muslim Background: A Global Census." *Interdisciplinary Journal of Research on Religion*, 11, Article 10, 1–19.

Momen, M. (1982). "The Trial of Mullā ʿAlī Basṭāmī: A Combined Sunnī-Shīʿī Fatwā against the Bāb." *Iran*, 20(1), 113–43.

Momen, M. (1983). "The Social Basis of the Bābī Upheavals in Iran (1848–53): A Preliminary Analysis." *International Journal of Middle East Studies*, 15(2), 157–83.

Momen, M. (2008a). "Millennialism and Violence: The Attempted Assassination of Nasir al-Din Shah of Iran by the Babis in 1852." *Nova Religio*, 12(1), 57–82.

Momen, M. (2008b). "The Baha'is and the Constitutional Revolution: The Case of Sari, Mazandaran, 1906–1913." *Iranian Studies*, 41(3), 343–63.

Momen, M. (2012). "The Constitutional Movement and the Baha'is of Iran: The Creation of an 'Enemy Within.'" *British Journal of Middle Eastern Studies*, 39(3), 328–46.

Momen, M. (2018). "Millennialist Narrative and Apocalyptic Violence: The Case of the Babis of Iran." *Journal of the British Association for the Study of Religion*, 20, 1–18.

Najjar, F. M. (2000). "Islamic Fundamentalism and the Intellectuals: The Case of Nasr Hāmid Abu Zayd." *British Journal of Middle Eastern Studies*, 27(2), 177–200.

Niechciał, P. (2023). "The Contemporary Collective Identity of Zoroastrians in Tehran: Between the Strategies of Dichotomization and Complementarization." In S. B. Hosseini, ed., *Ethnic Religious Minorities in Iran*. Singapore: Palgrave Macmillan, pp. 201–27.

Nikookar, H., and Hemmatpour, B. (2012). *Tars az Jurm*. Tehran: Nashr-i Mīzān.

Nowak, M. (2005). *U.N. Covenant on Civil and Political Rights: CCPR Commentary*, 2nd ed. Kehl: N. P. Engel.

Nyhagen, L., Halsaa, B. (2016). *Religion, Gender and Citizenship: Women of Faith, Gender Equality and Feminism*. London: Palgrave Macmillan.

Olson, P. J. (2006). "The Public Perception of 'Cults' and 'New Religious Movements.'" *Journal for the Scientific Study of Religion*, 45(1), 97–106.

Omelicheva, M. Y. (2016). "Islam and Power Legitimation: Instrumentalisation of Religion in Central Asian States." *Contemporary Politics*, 22(2), 144–63.

Paloutzian, R. F., Richardson, J. T., Rambo, L. R. (1999). "Religious Conversion and Personality Change." *Journal of Personality*, 67(6), 1047–79.

Philpott, D. (2019). *Religious Freedom in Islam: The Fate of a Universal Human Right in the Muslim World Today*. New York: Oxford University Press.

Philpott, D., and Shah, T. S. (2017). "In Response to Persecution: Essays from the Under Caesar's Sword Project." *Review of Faith & International Affairs*, 15(1), 1–11.

Philpott, D., and Shah, T. S. (2018). "Introduction." In D. Philpott and T. S. Shah, eds., *Under Caesar's Sword: How Christians Respond to Persecution*. Cambridge: Cambridge University Press, pp. 1–29.

Pink, J. (2003). "A Post-Qurʾan ic Religion between Apostasy and Public Order: Egyptian Muftis and Courts on the Legal Status of the Bahāʾī Faith." *Islamic Law and Society*, 10(3), 409–34.

Pistor-Hatam, A. (2021). "Freedom of Religion in the Islamic Republic of Iran and the 'Right to Have Rights.'" In A. Pistor-Hatam, ed., *Menschenrechte in der Islamischen Republik Iran*. Baden-Baden: Ergon, pp. 213–32.

Rad Goudarzi, M., and Najafinejad, A. (2019). "Necessity of Reinterpretation of Sharia in the Thoughts of a Grand Ayatollah: Saanei's Response to the Challenge of Human Rights in Islam." *Muslim World Journal of Human Rights*, 16(1), 27–49.

Ramazani, R. K. (1980). "Constitution of the Islamic Republic of Iran." *Middle East Journal*, 34(2), 181–204.

Ramezani Tamijani, S. (2016). ʿIlal wa Zamīnih-hā-yi Girāyish bi Maʿnawīyat-girāyī-yi Jadīd dar Iran. PhD Dissertation, Allameh Tabataba'i University, Tehran.

Ramezani Tamijani, S. (2020). *Maʿnawīyat-i bī-Sāmān: Taʾammulī Jāmiʿih-shinākhtī bar Maʿnawīyat-girāyī-yi Jadīd wa Chirāyī-yi Girāyish bi Ān dar Iran*. Tehran: Shirkat-i Chāp wa Nashr-i Bayn al-milal.

Raza, F. (2020). "Limitations to the Right to Religious Freedom: Rethinking Key Approaches." *Oxford Journal of Law and Religion*, 9(3), 435–62.

Rezaei, F. (2019). *Iran's Foreign Policy after the Nuclear Agreement: Politics of Normalizers and Traditionalists*. Cham: Palgrave Macmillan.

Richardson, J. T. (1993a). "Definitions of Cult: From Sociological-Technical to Popular-Negative." *Review of Religious Research*, 34(4), 348–56.

Richardson, J. T. (1993b). "A Social Psychological Critique of 'Brainwashing' Claims about Recruitment to New Religions." In J. K. Hadden and D. G. Bromley, eds., *The Handbook of Cults and Sects in America*. Greenwich, CT: JAI Press, pp. 75–97.

Richardson, J. T. (1995). "Minority Religions, Religious Freedom, and the New Pan-European Political and Judicial Institutions." *Journal of Church and State*, 37(1), 39–59.

Richardson, J. T. (2006). "The Sociology of Religious Freedom: A Structural and Socio-Legal Analysis." *Sociology of Religion*, 67(3), 271–94.

Richardson, J. T. (2007). "Religion, Law, and Human Rights." In P. Beyer and L. Beaman, eds., *Religion, Globalization, and Culture*. Leiden: Brill, pp. 407–28.

Richardson, J. T. (2014). "'Brainwashing' as Forensic Evidence." In S. J. Morewitz and M. L. Goldstein, eds., *Handbook of Forensic Sociology and Psychology*. New York: Springer, pp. 77–85.

Richardson, J. T. (2015). "Managing Religion and the Judicialization of Religious Freedom." *Journal for the Scientific Study of Religion*, 54(1), 1–19.

Richardson, J. T. (2019). "Religious Freedom in Flux: The European Court of Human Rights Grapples with Ethnic, Cultural, Religious, and Legal Pluralism." *Changing Societies & Personalities*, 3(4), 303–18.

Richardson, J. T. (2021). "The Judicialization of Religious Freedom: Variations on a Theme." *Social Compass*, 68(3), 375–91.

Richardson, J. T. (2023). "Contradictions, Conflicts, Dilemmas, and Temporary Resolutions: A Sociology of Law Analysis of *Shari'a* in Selected Western Societies." In A. Possamai, J. T. Richardson, and B. S. Turner, eds., *The*

Sociology of Shari'a: Case Studies from around the World, 2nd ed., Cham: Springer, pp. 303–24.

Richardson, J. T., and Adeliyan Tous, S. (2023). "'Brainwashing' and Mental Health: An Update." In H. S. Friedman and C. H. Markey, eds., *Encyclopedia of Mental Health*. Vol. 1, 3rd ed. London: Academic Press (Elsevier), pp. 290–7.

Richardson, J. T., and McGraw, B. (2019). "Congressional Efforts to Defend and Extend Religious Freedom and the Law of Unintended Consequences." *Religion–Staat–Gesellschaft*, 20(1–2), 33–48.

Robertson, R. (2007). "Global Millennialism: A Postmortem on Secularization." In P. Beyer and L. Beaman, eds., *Religion, Globalization and Culture*. Leiden: Brill, pp. 9–34.

Robertson, R. (2009). "Globalization, Theocratization, and Politicized Civil Religion." In P. B. Clarke, ed., *The Oxford Handbook of the Sociology of Religion*. Oxford: Oxford University Press, pp. 451–77.

Sachedina, A. (2009). *Islam and the Challenge of Human Rights*. Oxford: Oxford University Press.

Sadeghnia, M. (2020). "Maʿnawīyat-hā-yi Jadīd bi Mathābih-yi Masʾalih-ī Jāmiʿih-shinākhtī." In H. Vakili and A. Shakernejad, eds., *Majmūʿih-yi Maqālāt-i Hamāyish-i Millī-yi Maʿnawīyat-hā-yi Nuw-ẓuhūr: Shākhiṣih-hā wa Naqd-hā*. Qom: Islamic Sciences and Culture Academy, pp. 287–311.

Saeedi, M. (2022). "Taḥawwulāt-i Dīnī dar Dunyā-yi Muʿāṣir bā Taʾkīd bar Dīn-hā wa Maʿnawīyat-hā-yi Jadīd." *Muṭāliʿāt-i Jāmiʿih-shināsī*, 15(2), 161–83.

Saiedi, N. (2022). "The Writings and Teachings of the Báb." In R. H. Stockman, ed., *The World of the Baháʾí Faith*. London: Routledge, pp. 29–39.

Sanasarian, E. (2000). *Religious Minorities in Iran*. Cambridge: Cambridge University Press.

Sanyal, A. (2019). "Baha'is in Post-Revolution Iran: Perspectives of the Ulema." *Contemporary Review of the Middle East*, 6(1), 58–74.

Sarkissian, A. (2015). *The Varieties of Religious Repression: Why Governments Restrict Religion*. New York: Oxford University Press.

Schirazi, A. (1997). *The Constitution of Iran: Politics and the State in the Islamic Republic*. Translated by J. O'Kane. London: I. B. Tauris.

Scott, J., and Marshall, G. (2009). *A Dictionary of Sociology*, 3rd revised ed. Oxford: Oxford University Press.

Shariʿati Mazinani, S. (2008). "Preface." In J. Cresswell and B. Wilson, eds., *New Religious Movements: Challenge and Response*. Translated by M. Gholipour. Mashhad: Nashr-i Marandīz, pp. 11–13.

Shahvar, S. (2009). "The Islamic Regime in Iran and Its Attitude towards the Jews: The Religious and Political Dimensions." *Immigrants & Minorities*, 27 (1), 82–117.

Sharifi, A. (2013). *Darʾāmadī bar ʿIrfān-i Ḥaqīqī wa ʿIrfān-hā-yi Kādhib*, 12th printing. Qom: Partuw-i Wilāyat.

Sharifi-doost, H. (2020). *Kāwushī dar Maʿnawīyat-hā-yi Nuw-ẓuhūr: Barrasī-yi Dah Jaryān-i Faʿʿāl dar Iran*. Qom: Daftar-i Nashr-i Maʿārif.

Sharifiyan, A. (2018). "Chālishī bi Nām-i 'Qānūn-i Ḍidd-i Firqih': Nigāhī bi Sīyāsat-hā-yi Muqābilih-ī-yi Kishwar-hā-yi Mukhtalif bā Firqih-hā-yi Inḥirāfī." *Ruwshanā: Faṣlnāmih-yi Takhaṣṣuṣī-yi Firaq wa Adyān*, 9(2), 106–10.

Sheikh, M. Z. H., and Ahmed, Z. S. (2020). "Military, Authoritarianism and Islam: A Comparative Analysis of Bangladesh and Pakistan." *Politics and Religion*, 13(2), 333–60.

Shih, C. (1999). *Collective Democracy: Political and Legal Reform in China*. Hong Kong: Chinese University Press.

Smith, A. (1937). *An Inquiry into the Nature and Causes of the Wealth of Nations*. New York: The Modern Library.

Stark, R., and Finke, R. (2000). *Acts of Faith: Explaining the Human Side of Religion*. Berkeley: University of California Press.

Stausberg, M. (2012). "From Power to Powerlessness: Zoroastrianism in Iranian History." In A. Nga Longva and A. Sofie Roald, eds., *Religious Minorities in the Middle East: Domination, Self-Empowerment, Accommodation*. Leiden: Brill, pp. 171–94.

Talebi Darabi, B. (2012). Firqih-girāyī-yi Jadīd dar Iran: Taḥlīl-i Jāmiʿih-shinākhtī-yi ʿIrfān-hā-yi Nuw-ẓuhūr dar Iran. PhD Dissertation, Allameh Tabataba'i University, Tehran.

Tamadonfar, M., and Lewis, R. B. (2020). "Religious Regulation in Iran." In P. A. Djupe, M. J. Rozell, and T. G. Jelen, eds., *The Oxford Encyclopedia of Politics and Religion*. New York: Oxford University Press, pp. 1373–90.

Tamanaha, B. Z. (2005). "The Tension between Legal Instrumentalism and the Rule of Law." *Syracuse Journal of International Law and Commerce*, 33(1), 131–54.

Tamanaha, B. Z. (2006a). *The Perils of Pervasive Legal Instrumentalism*. Nijmegen: Wolf Legal.

Tamanaha, B. Z. (2006b). *Law as a Means to an End: Threat to the Rule of Law*. Cambridge: Cambridge University Press.

Tamanaha, B. Z. (2007). "How an Instrumental View of Law Corrodes the Rule of Law." *DePaul Law Review*, 56(2), 469–505.

Tate, C. N., and Vallinder, T. (1995). *The Global Expansion of Judicial Power*. New York: New York University Press.

Tavakoli-Targhi, M. (2008). "Anti-Bahaʾism and Islamism in Iran." In D. P. Brookshaw and S. B. Fazel, eds., *The Bahaʾis of Iran: Socio-Historical Studies*. London: Routledge, pp. 200–31.

Tellenbach, S. (2013). "The Principle of Legality in the Iranian Constitutional and Criminal Law." In S. A. Arjomand and N. J. Brown, eds., *The Rule of Law, Islam, and Constitutional Politics in Egypt and Iran*. Albany: State University of New York Press, pp. 101–22.

Uddin, A. T. (2013). "A Legal Analysis of Ahmadi Persecution in Pakistan." In D. M. Kirkham, ed., *State Responses to Minority Religions*. London: Routledge, pp. 81–97.

UN Doc. (1982). *Report of the Human Rights Committee, General Assembly, 39th Session*. Supplement No. 40 (A/37/40). 22 September.

UN Doc. (1984). *Summary Record of the 65th Meeting, 3rd Committee, Held on Friday, 7 December 1984, General Assembly, 39th Session*. A/C.3/39/SR.65. December 17.

UN Doc. (1991a). *Report on the Human Rights Situation in the Islamic Republic of Iran by the Special Representative of the Commission on Human Rights, Mr. Reynaldo Galindo Pohl, pursuant to Commission Resolution 1990/79*. E/CN.4/1991/35. 13 February.

UN Doc. (1991b). *Implementation of the Declaration on the Elimination of All Forms of Intolerance and of Discrimination based on Religion or Belief: Report Submitted by Mr. Angelo Vidal d'Almeida Ribeiro, Special Rapporteur Appointed in Accordance with Commission on Human Rights Resolution 1986/20 of 10 March 1986*. E/CN.4/1991/56. 18 January.

UN Doc. (1993). *Final Report on the Situation of Human Rights in the Islamic Republic of Iran by the Special Representative of the Commission on Human Rights, Mr. Reynaldo Galindo Pohl, pursuant to Commission Resolution 1992/67 of 4 March 1992*. E/CN.4/1993/41. 28 January.

UN Doc. (2014). *Report of the Special Rapporteur on Freedom of Religion or Belief, Heiner Bielefeldt*. A/HRC/28/66/Add.1. December 23.

UN Doc. (2019). *Situation of Human Rights in the Islamic Republic of Iran: Report of the Special Rapporteur on the Situation of Human Rights in the Islamic Republic of Iran, Note by the Secretary-General*. A/74/188. 18 July.

UN Doc. (2022). *Report of the Special Rapporteur on the Situation of Human Rights in the Islamic Republic of Iran, Javaid Rehman*. A/HRC/49/75. 13 January.

Vahman, F. (2019). *175 Years of Persecution: A History of the Babis & Baha'is of Iran*. London: Oneworld.

Vallinder, T. (1994). "The Judicialization of Politics—A World-wide Phenomenon: Introduction." *International Political Science Review*, 15(2), 91–9.

Van der Vyver, J. D. (2005). "Limitations of Freedom of Religion or Belief: International Law Perspectives." *Emory International Law Review*, 11(2), 499–538.

Van Gorder, C. (2018). "Christian Responses to Persecution in the Islamic Republic of Iran and the Kingdom of Saudi Arabia." In D. Philpott and T. S. Shah, eds., *Under Caesar's Sword: How Christians Respond to Persecution*. Cambridge: Cambridge University Press, pp. 130–61.

Voltaire. (1894). *Letters On England*. London: Cassell and Company Limited.

Walbridge, J. (1996). "The Babi Uprising in Zanjan: Causes and Issues." *Iranian Studies*, 29(3–4), 339–62.

Yazdani, M. (2011). Religious Contentions in Modern Iran, 1881–1941. PhD Dissertation, University of Toronto.

Yazdani, M. (2012). "The Islamic Revolution's Internal Other: The Case of Ayatollah Khomeini and the Baha'is of Iran." *Journal of Religious History*, 36(4), 593–604.

Yazdani, M. (2015). "Higher Education under the Islamic Republic: The Case of the Baha'is." *Journal of Educational Controversy*, 10(1), Article No. 7, 1–19.

Yazdani, M. (2017). "Towards a History of Iran's Baha'i Community During the Reign of Mohammad Reza Shah, 1941–1979." *Iran Namag*, 2(1), 156–81.

Yazdani, M. (2018). "Quiet Strangulation: Islamic Republic's Treatment of Baha'is Since 1991." *Tiempo Devorado*, 5(2), 66–93.

Zabihi-Moghaddam, S. (2002). "The Babi-State Conflict at Shaykh Tabarsi." *Iranian Studies*, 35(1–3), 87–112.

Zabihi-Moghaddam, S. (2016). "State-Sponsored Persecution of Baha'is in the Islamic Republic of Iran." *Contemporary Review of the Middle East*, 3(2), 124–46.

Zainol, N. Z. N., Abd Majid, L., and Kadir, M. N. A. (2014). "Nasr Hamid Abu Zayd as a Modern Muslim Thinker." *International Journal of Islamic Thought*, 5(1), 61–70.

Zatz, M. S. (1994). *Producing Legality: Law and Socialism in Cuba*. New York: Routledge.

Cambridge Elements

New Religious Movements

Founding Editor

† James R. Lewis

Wuhan University

The late James R. Lewis was Professor of Philosophy at Wuhan University, China. He served as the editor or co-editor for four book series, was the general editor for the *Alternative Spirituality and Religion Review*, and the associate editor for the *Journal of Religion and Violence*. His publications include *The Cambridge Companion to Religion and Terrorism* (Cambridge University Press 2017) and *Falun Gong: Spiritual Warfare and Martyrdom* (Cambridge University Press 2018).

Series Editor

Rebecca Moore

San Diego State University

Rebecca Moore is Emerita Professor of Religious Studies at San Diego State University. She has written and edited numerous books and articles on Peoples Temple and the Jonestown tragedy. She has served as co-general editor or reviews editor of *Nova Religio* since 2000. Publications include *Beyond Brainwashing: Perspectives on Cult Violence* (Cambridge University Press 2018) and *Peoples Temple and Jonestown in the Twenty-First Century* (Cambridge University Press 2022).

About the Series

Elements in New Religious Movements go beyond cult stereotypes and popular prejudices to present new religions and their adherents in a scholarly and engaging manner. Case studies of individual groups, such as Transcendental Meditation and Scientology, provide in-depth consideration of some of the most well known, and controversial, groups. Thematic examinations of women, children, science, technology, and other topics focus on specific issues unique to these groups. Historical analyses locate new religions in specific religious, social, political, and cultural contexts. These examinations demonstrate why some groups exist in tension with the wider society and why others live peaceably in the mainstream. The series highlights the differences, as well as the similarities, within this great variety of religious expressions. To discuss contributing to this series please contact Professor Moore, remoore@sdsu.edu.

Cambridge Elements

New Religious Movements

Elements in the series

Hare Krishna in the Twenty-First Century
Angela R. Burt

The Christian Countercult Movement
Douglas E. Cowan

Shamanic Materialities in Nordic Climates
Trude Fonneland and Tiina Äikäs

Communal Societies and New Religious Movements
Cheryl Coulthard

Satanism
Joseph P. Laycock

Fieldwork in New Religious Movements
George D. Chryssides

New Religious Movements and Comparative Religion
Olav Hammer and Karen Swartz

The New Witches of the West
Ethan Doyle White

The New Age Movement
Margrethe Løøv

Black Hebrew Israelites
Michael T. Miller

Managing Religion and Religious Changes in Iran: A Socio-Legal Analysis
Sajjad Adeliyan Tous and James T. Richardson

A full series listing is available at: www.cambridge.org/ENRM